Acknowledgements

THE author wishes to record his thanks to all those who have helped him with both the original and this present revised edition. In particular, he would mention John Spencer and Tom Webb. Peter Drucker, the distinguished writer on management subjects, was specially helpful when the book was first mooted in the early sixties. The author is also grateful to those named companies who have supplied material for case histories. Finally, he would like to record a special word of thanks to his publisher who has shown sustained enthusiasm for the project.

D0773825

Essere humano

Federigo da Montefeltro
(Lord of Urbino 1444-1482)
on good government.

Introduction to the Fourth Edition

WHEN the writer sat down nearly a decade ago to write the first edition of this book on management the turbulence and uncertainties which colour these closing years of the sixties, and which had followed the end of the 1939–1945 war, seemed somewhat muted. The Suez crisis was not long past and, with it, inevitable apprehensions about another world disaster. But it looked, in 1960, as if some good sense had been learnt and as if Britain's urgent tasks were to be in the field of ensuring economic stability and associating that stability with the search for a new role in world affairs, the necessity for which the Suez débacle had all too vividly revealed. It seemed indeed, and has seemed so to the writer ever since, that, as technology advances, management becomes the key factor for Britain's survival. Or perhaps survival is too emotive a word. It is, rather, the key factor if Britain is to hold her own, to achieve industrial, agricultural and commercial growth and, above all, if she is to replace her old leadership with new and enduring values of a possibly different kind from the former accepted ones. This is a harrassed and complex world and Britain has much to offer.

As edition has followed edition over the years, the writer's gratitude for the encouragingly wide interest in what he tried to say has been tempered with the knowledge that so much still remains to be said. There is, in any study of the business of management, no point at which it can be claimed that the last, definitive, words have been written. While revising the text as well as arranging new and up-dated case histories, the writer has had it closely in mind that management is forever on the move. What can only be described as a massive acceleration in the pace of the provision of the means for scientific management has been the most significant development since the book's first appearance in 1961. It is with the underlining of this fact that this new edition is largely concerned.

This book is neither a manual nor a textbook. It would be presumptuous to attempt such an exercise. As the text unfolds it will be obvious to the reader that the only management lesson the writer has learnt over a good many years of managing and being managed is that management 'rules' must always be subordinated to wider, human issues. It is only when management behaviour can strike a balance between what is both humanly and technically valid that a relationship between manager and managed emerges which is, to put it bluntly, of the least imperfect kind. And even at this point in the somewhat daunting adventure in exposition which lies before the writer he can see clouds on the horizon. Humanly? Technically? What do these two words really mean? Who is in a position to judge a 'human' situation? In Russia and China there are management strategies being applied at the moment which are inimical to Western ideas. Are they the more or less 'human' if set against the problems and historical background of both those countries' commercial, agricultural, and political development in this century? Or the word 'technical'? There are a hundred shades of meaning to this essentially contemporary word. To draw any glib technical conclusion – or, rather, to assume that a particular management action is necessarily technically right – could often be very wide of the mark.

The fact remains that in both sophisticated and primitive societies – and, more important still, in emergent societies – there will always be managers and managed. The Chief of an African tribe, a Politician, a Managing Director, a Foreman, a Headmaster – all are manifestations, chosen at random, of man's seemingly unchanging desire to range behind some sort of leader who will accept responsibility – who will, in fact, manage.

That there is such tremendous preoccupation today with the art (or craft) of management suggests that very few of the stable conditions against which management practices used to flourish now apply, and, with the greatest respect to an impressive body of writing on management subjects, much of the background against which this writing was produced no longer exists.

Thus there is much heart-searching as to what management is now all about. The African Chief finds himself borne along on a tide of demagogy. The Politician is at the mercy of the so-called 'free' Press. The Managing Director is told that the profit motive – a good enough motivation in the old days – is now somehow anti-social. The Foreman is inhibited by the Unions. The Headmaster is intimidated by the parent.

These are not fanciful assumptions: we see all round us today in this articulate age a complex of changing values, and the manager's dilemma is whether to go on doing what he knows, according to standards he has accepted and understood, or to try to meet the distinctive challenges of his rapidly shifting environment.

It would be very tempting to write a book which dealt with management in all its aspects, for if it is true that there will always be those who must lead and those who must be led it would be fascinating to speculate on such a theme and relate it to every form of human endeavour. But that is not what this book is going to try to do. Rather, it will take management in the narrower but urgent and topical context of business, and attempt to stimulate thought about an activity which is basic to the achievement of satisfaction among a great and growing number of people.

There is a need, however, before the examination begins, to be clear about what is meant by 'business'. As Toynbee has wisely said, it is too general to think of business as working to earn one's living. Most of the world has to do that. He suggests that business means trade, finance, and industry, and that in industry it is usually considered that the business people are not so much the workers in the factories as the workers in the offices from which industries are managed. But there is a paradox here. Business has traditionally meant employment for gain, as well as work which is not carried out for remuneration received from an employer in the form of wage or salary, but profit earned by a worker by his own enterprise and initiative. The paradox lies in the fact that today very few businessmen actually work for profit. Toynbee asks if it is not true that the great majority of people today engaged in business, are, in fact, employees and, as such, are in the same position as employees in the factory.

He is surely right. It is precisely because of this diffusion of the business function, of which the 'managerial revolution' is one striking consequence, that there is no short cut to evolving what might be called 'conclusions and recommendations' in the matter of business management. The business net is capacious and contains within it today fish as large as the financier who operates on a bewilderingly complicated scale and minnows as small as the girl on a loom, or perhaps more relevant, the man or woman who puts the parma violet on the chocolate cream. It includes also the, possibly diminishing but still considerable, number of self-employed, as well as the number of smaller businesses in which the profit motive is not so remote.

Size is also a characteristic which must put anyone who sets out to discuss business management on his guard. Huge industrial complexes like Unilever or I.C.I. inevitably pose different problems from the middle-sized engineering firm, the departmental store, or the small family business. Clearly, in considering any one of the many aspects of business management, allowance has to be made, not only for the size and character of a business, but for the nature of the business itself and the changes it will be going through as the technological era develops. There is a danger, in a book of this kind, in enunciating principles and philosophies which have only a very limited application.

But some principles and philosophies are better than none at all. Management practice has tended to grow in a very haphazard way and, in Great Britain particularly, it is surprising how comparatively little public attention has been paid to a subject which, of its very nature, strikes at the heart of social behaviour.

Only in very recent times has there been an upsurge in business training in this country. This is epitomized by the establishment of the London and Manchester Business Schools and the fact that there is a growing movement towards the 'professionalization' of management is one indication of how some people in Britain are thinking. This poses some sizable problems for this book. Should it attempt to examine management outside the author's field of experience – which is inevitably mainly in Britain and the Commonwealth? Are there, in fact, such great differences between North America (where the Harvard Business School, to take but one example, has established a great reputation) and the rest of the free world as to warrant making constant reservations?

There is fortunately today a good deal of getting together on management subjects, and it would be broadly true to say that, so far as Western Europe and North America are concerned, the gap between management practices is narrowing. It will also be remembered how revealing were the visits of the sixty-seven teams which visited the U.S.A. during the years 1949–53 under the management of the Anglo-American Productivity Council. A chain reaction was started which still continues to gather strength. Nevertheless this book, it must be fairly stated, will tend to deal in greater depth with Britain's situation than with those of her neighbours. In any case the aim of full employment has produced a national commitment to, and preoccupation with, a declared objective which gives a keen edge to the management problem and which makes our British situation the more challenging.

The most pressing question of our day is to solve the agonizing problem of how man is to live and work with man without exterminating the species in the process. Enlightened leadership in management, whether the readers' verdict be that it is an art, a craft, a technique, a science, or a humanity – or a mixture of the lot – can play a decisive part in resolving the problem of human survival.

I

The Business of Business

OVER ten years ago the Harvard Business School had completed fifty years of existence and a conference of some two thousand business people was called together to consider how management was meeting the challenges of these times. Some twenty extremely provocative addresses, together with a certain amount of discussion, were subsequently published in a remarkable book called *Management's Mission in a New Society*, and it is particularly interesting that the first address of all, the pace-setter as it were, was by the only Englishman to speak, Arnold Toynbee, under the title 'How Did we Get this Way – and Where are we Going?' – interesting because, as the opening section in a later chapter will show, Europe (and Britain especially) has since the last war presented management with a host of entirely new problems. At Harvard, business leaders, statesmen, teachers, and observers were deeply concerned with problems ranging from national security to power and morality in business and asking themselves questions, not about the day-to-day practices of management, but, so much more complex and baffling, the 'whys': what, in fact, the business of business is; what is it all about? A book about management, however speculatively, indeed diffidently, it tackles it, must try to answer the question.

Out of what must have been millions of words uttered with varying degrees of passion during those two important days in 1958 came a definition which is stimulating enough to warrant quotation and is accepted almost unquestioned. It was that businesses exist to create and deliver value satisfactions at a profit. However much such a definition can be argued or adjusted, it contains within it the heart of business matter. The profitable creation of a market (and markets are people) must be and always will be the *raison d'être* of a business. Profit-making, though put at the end of the definition, is obviously as much a part of the business function as producing goods or services or distributing them, but in present-day trading conditions the relation of profit to the total business operation has considerably altered. This new relationship will be reviewed later in this chapter, but at this point it would be relevant to add that the 'profit motive' no longer dominates business thinking. Clearly, in the preliminary planning of any enterprise, profit is a motivation, and it would be naïve to suggest otherwise. But if a detailed study were to be made of all the factors that go to the birth of a business, the 'creative' one would probably emerge every bit as strongly as the more obvious desire to make a profit. In any case this chapter is considering the *purpose* of business: it is arguable whether profit as such is as much a business purpose as so many accountants and economists would have the world believe. Another factor which must bear on the profit question is the growth of the public sector of business activity. Nationalized industries, with all too rare exceptions, have long since forgotten the word profit.

It would be well to analyse the question of customer-creating a little more thoroughly, because it must be admitted that in Britain this has been belatedly recognized as a business purpose. Markets do not happen by chance. They are the result of the business action which anticipates a need. This is not to say that the want that is satisfied may not have been already felt; but until someone has the enterprise to meet it the desire is often unexpressed and vague. Equally, it can be that a business action starts from scratch and creates a want; in Britain who would have dreamed a few years ago that Carnaby Street would have become an international symbol?

A topical example of the question of both satisfying hitherto dimly felt but unsatisfied want as well as *creating* a want is the supply of consumer goods to the so-called undeveloped countries. It is a fascinating exercise to probe a little into, say, the wants of cash-crop cultivators – small, independent growers of coffee and cotton, for example – in an African community. Here are men and women who, because of the growth of world demand for cotton and coffee under normal conditions, are no longer victims of a near-subsistence economy. They have money to spend; but it is business enterprise – whether it is local effort or the imaginative energy of men thousands of miles away in London, Manchester, or New York – that can alone turn that money into what the definition under discussion calls 'value satisfaction'. And, parenthetically, it must be added that precious opportunities in these fields of business are being lost by Britain.

Carnaby Street for 'with it' youngsters and motor-cars or radios for African farmers are only small signals pointing to a far larger question. Businesses can only survive if those responsible for them realize that what they think they produce – whether goods or services – is of less importance than what the consumer thinks he or she is consuming. The prosperity of a business depends on the sense of 'value satisfaction' enjoyed by the customer. The Rowntree case history in a later chapter 'Successful Management' vividly illustrates this point.

A section in a later chapter will consider the detailed management of marketing and how, synthesized with production and finance, it completes the business 'trinity' – the three chief *means* by which management achieves its objectives. In the present context marketing has a far wider meaning. If the business of business is to create a customer, then marketing and inventiveness ('innovation' as some American writers call it) distinguish business from other forms of human undertaking. When goods or services are produced, distributed, and sold, a business comes into being. It could be argued here that there are other activities, never before considered in the same breath as 'business', that are becoming dependent on this wider concept of marketing for their success. The Church, for example, may be said to be marketing a service, and it needs, possibly more urgently today than ever before, to go out and sell itself. Or the Army which tries to present a favourable public image with the object of increasing recruitment. Or the nationalized industries, which are in competition with private enterprise for both staff and customers. In any case routine marketing techniques, such as market research and analysis, are surely applicable to any form of enterprise involving the creation and delivery of 'value satisfaction', whether material or spiritual.

But this is perhaps to take the business function outside the field under discussion. Basically the business of business has to do with goods and services which meet material needs, and any enterprise in which really aggressive marketing and inventiveness are only supernumerary activities can hardly be called a business.

It is not surprising that this marketing function has, in Britain at least, taken so long to be understood as one of two main business purposes. For decades in this country a stigma has somehow attached itself to selling. 'Look out for Joe, he'd sell you anything' or '*caveat emptor*' were almost national slogans. Production and finance have long since been highly respectable. Marketing is somehow ungentlemanly.

This is of course rapidly changing. The old story 'it's up to the sales department to sell what we make' is becoming whiskered but, even so, it is no exaggeration that unless a business has within it a clear conception of marketing – customer creation – as the policy to be considered at the very start of the planning for the launching of a product or service, there will be no health in it. In Britain, although he situation is improving, those men and women with marketing vision, seeing it as the unique and central function of a business, are all too rare. And it is precisely because of the importance of the marketing job that has to be done that, at last, marketing is earning its proper place at the top of the management hierarchy. It is not enough, any longer, to tack marketing on to the end of the sales department; it has to span the entire business operation; it has to feed the researcher, the planner, the designer, the engineer, just as much as the salesman and the sales promoter. How can a customer be created if, from the word 'go', the needs of that customer (who after all is the market) are not in the forefront of the planning?

It follows that dynamic marketing is of little value in an economic vacuum. Business can only flourish when the economy is on the move, and therefore inventiveness or innovation must be regarded as the second basic business function. What is meant by these words? Broadly the answer is that the business of business, in addition to creating customers, must be to provide more efficient – or better and more economic – goods and services. Whether it is a question of inventiveness or innovation, the implication is clear: every branch of a business activity must be for ever on the alert to discover ways and means of improving, changing, enriching the total operation. These words all underline the implicit dynamism in the business of business. Like marketing, this need to think ahead is not confined to any one of the aspects of the business. What a product offers to the customer needs frequent reassessment, from design to engineering to distribution to price. And a service just as much as a product can never be said to be totally adequate under any conditions, because conditions themselves are constantly changing. Thus, for example, the insurance business must be ready to introduce new forms of cover or a bank new forms of loan to meet or, better, to anticipate *customer* demands. Business, in a word, exists to see the whole of a market and to bend its organization, its inventiveness, and its powers of innovation to meeting it. Did not Gibbon write 'all that is human must retrograde if it does not advance'?

The foregoing has looked at business in a straightforward, commercial context. 'Value satisfaction' puts the onus on the customer. If the customer does not think he is getting value for his atomic reactor, his automated warehouse, his breakfast cereal, or his cigarette, he probably won't buy it – or he certainly won't buy again. But something else – a new philosophy of business, as it were – has emerged, especially since the last war. 'Value satisfaction' has extended back from the customer to the worker, and here the emphasis is on the word 'satisfaction'. It is not enough today for a business to direct its energies solely to creating and satisfying customers, though that is the priority. The crude lessons of the Industrial Revolution are now being learnt, and today, whether business likes it or not, there is a secondary consideration, every bit as real and every bit as potent. It is to ensure a degree of satisfaction to the worker, whatever his grade, who is employed in the business enterprise. The aggregate achievement of the Trade Union movement (which will be considered in a later chapter) and the national commitment to a policy of full employment mean that the business of business is no longer *only* a question of looking outwards. The definition set down at the start of this chapter needs, then, a second look. Business, it is true, exists for a main purpose – to create and deliver value satisfaction at a profit. But it is clear that those value satisfactions can only be created and delivered if the business itself is an enlightened employer. This is not to say that there are many instances of business enterprises which, in a fever of anxiety to catch the customer's penny or pound, supply a market requirement with complete disregard of conditions of employment. Such enterprises are, today, short-lived.

The new business 'philosophy' has also to battle with another question. It is not enough any longer to create a demand and to supply it with second-rate merchandise or services. The responsibility of business in this field is immense. A good deal of the current heart-searching in the United States stems from a reconsideration of the 'value' part in the expression 'value satisfaction'. Erwin Canham, Editor of the *Christian Science Monitor*, has spoken of '. . . the tawdry materialism of conspicuous consumption, spread by the mass media, accompanied by rock 'n' roll, spluttered by comic books . . . the symbol of America in most of the world' and, elsewhere, 'what has inverted our values? For one thing we have deified production for production's sake. There is nothing wrong with the increased production of consumer goods, but there is a great deal wrong in thinking and acting as if the mere production of goods were a justifiable social goal. . . .'

In Britain 'conspicuous consumption' is a pretty new idea. 'Poverty of desire', as Ernest Bevin once put it when considering the galaxy of goods in America and comparing it with the British resistance to innovation, is no longer apparent. Many more people now want more things. It is estimated, for example, that the teenager market – unmarried youngsters in Britain between sixteen and twenty-three – has well over £1,000 million to spend annually. But British business – and this thought is developed in a later chapter when discussing management for the consumer – is in danger of falling into the trap in which much of American business is currently caught. Inadequate standards of performance, poor design, shoddy, catchpenny goods, totally misleading advertising claims, and a preoccupation with obsolescence: these are but four examples of what can happen if business is not self-disciplined.

This brief discussion of the business of business has still to concern itself with two other factors which are relevant: they are productivity and profits, and each of them properly calls for a book on its own. Productivity, as is so often said nowadays, is an attitude of mind. It is not to be confused with production which is a fact. Though, by definition, productivity means the better use of all available resources, be they of men, machines, or money, 'better use' implies the existence within a business of an attitude towards its operations which is dominated by the *will* to do better. It is the means to a fuller life for an even greater number of people and it is not, as seems to be so often assumed, simply a question of getting more out of a labour force.

Productivity is in any case no longer only concerned with manufacturing, with the substitution of muscle by mind. It ranges into all business activity, including management, and notably that of distribution. The definition at the beginning of this chapter spoke not only of the creation but the 'delivering' – the distribution – of value satisfaction. Allowing for the reservations in the previous section, there is immense scope today for increasing productivity by distribution. Mass advertising media – press and television – create demand in advance of individual selling effort and, in many instances, more of the consumer's penny or pound goes on advertising than on the cost of production. In addition there are distributive means – self-service, the supermarket, selling by direct mail – which, in the field of consumer goods (which are, after all, most closely related to the 'fuller life'), can revolutionize business productivity.

A great deal today is being said and written about automation, which is another facet of productivity. There is much confused thinking about automation. It is not a nightmare of push-button machines and soul-destroying anonymity. It is, rather, a conception of how work should be organized. And work in this connexion is not just industrial production, but covers the whole business of business – distribution, clerical work in offices, financial controls, even planning. Of course there is gadgetry in automation and much focus on mechanization and controls, but essentially automation (which really symbolizes the new technology) pays little attention either to skills or to the product or service to be economically supplied. It takes far more notice of the undeniable fact that there are discernible *patterns* in most happenings. Automation takes these patterns and hammers out ways and means by which processes can be developed which will produce goods and services in the greatest variety, at the lowest cost, and with the least effort. This is a considerable simplification, but this hurdle of definition, even if many readers will find a hundred refinements of it, had to be jumped.

The business of business is today a great deal more, then, than making something or providing a service. The involvement is greater. It includes recognizing responsibilities inwards to workers; and, outwards, to setting a vigilant standard of production or service which will not debase the business function. This may sound pious and unreal, but if the principle of free enterprise is to survive, business cannot shut its eyes to this larger role. Time may be running out.

*

A final point to be considered is the question of profit or, as it has been well called, the avoidance of loss. A business cannot continue to exist if it loses money, or if the money it makes is not sufficient to buttress it against the normal risks that have to be taken. Furthermore, profit is required in order to underwrite the cost of expansion. If a business marks time it will soon be left far behind. Research and development, new machinery, new techniques of management which eliminate much of the guesswork – the dynamic approach, in fact, to marketing, inventiveness, and productivity which has been sketched out in this chapter – cost money. Additionally, a business, as will be developed later, has a considerable obligation to its shareholders.

But in Britain there is another, and very topical, aspect to this matter of profit. It has to do with the total national commitment to the maintenance of a welfare state – a welfare state which costs fabulous sums of money. This commitment can be financed only from taxation, direct and indirect, and the contribution by business enterprise to it is binding and permanent. In the early part of this century and, effectively, up till the work of Lord Beveridge, only a fraction of the responsibility for the elimination of the worst aspects of poverty and social injustice was accepted by business groups. The community as a whole is now involved, and the biggest single contributor is business enterprise. Is it not then incumbent upon business, in its relation with society, ceaselessly to improve its profit-earning capacity, not only in order to develop its own operations, reward its shareholders, insure against risk, and keep reserves for expansion, but also to play its part in the securing of social objectives about which, today, there is precious little political disagreement? And it is not only the taxation on profits but the vast contribution in local taxation – rates and the like – which business is called upon to pay.

This book is not a political treatise. It does not seek to take sides in the argument of free enterprise against a socialized economy. Possibly the formula that Britain is painfully evolving – a reasonable compromise between freedom and control – works best for this country. But what is fundamental to the business of business is the fact that if a relatively 'free' economy is to be maintained in which consumer choice and full employment are concomitants, management becomes a matter of high importance. Inefficiency is self-destroying; the new business technologies which have been touched upon in this chapter place an ever greater emphasis of responsibility on those men and women, from top to bottom in the management structure, who have to take the decisions and give the lead. A scientific approach to management and the means for achieving it have had huge stimulus in recent years from the use of the computer. It is no exaggeration to say that business control and forward planning have been revolutionized as a result of being able to programme a flow of information accurately and speedily and draw therefrom material for making short and long term decisions.

2

Qualities of Management

THE purpose of this chapter and the one that follows, together with the opening of the discussion on 'How a Manager Manages', entitle the reader to a word of preliminary explanation. Writing about management raises a particular difficulty for both author and reader which is that, inevitably, technical and human aspects tend to overlap. It is not hard to see why. Management is essentially a human affair and this fact overshadows all other considerations. On the other hand, management is a job, and a highly technical one. This chapter will try, in the course of examining management qualities in the more human context, to resolve the point at which the technical qualities yield to the less tangible ones. In so doing it will become clear that the leadership quality, both in the manager himself and in the management process, is clearly the prime factor. Therefore a short chapter – somewhat speculative and searching – has been set aside from the main stream of the book in order to look at leadership in somewhat more abstract terms. At the beginning of the chapter which follows, and which has the more general heading 'The Business of Management', it has been necessary to proclaim once again the belief that all the formulae in the world can be of little use if human qualities, crystallizing into leadership, are lacking in the manager himself. But that can be no excuse for shirking the task of setting down, quite factually, something of the proven experience of managers who have done and are doing a testing job successfully.

*

In this matter of qualities of management there are no golden rules. Anyone who tries to dogmatize about this question is asking for certain trouble, because management circumstances are seldom, if ever, duplicated; indeed, the management challenge lies precisely in the ability to measure such circumstances against an ever-changing background of problems and personalities. An inflexible attitude (or, for that matter, a too flexible one) to the task of managing can be disastrous. Even so, there is no excuse for managers and managed not to try to think out those qualities which should be offered and sought in various conditions. What no writer on management subjects, however well-intentioned, can hope to do is to supply easy answers to a question which is largely intangible and personal.

In an ideal world the manager would possess all those qualities in abundant measure which are always considered in relation to managers. Able to think with crystal clarity, he would combine a thorough technical knowledge of the goods or services with which he is concerned with shining integrity, shrewdness, an enterprising and humane outlook, high intelligence, and considerable powers of leadership. And what an impossible bore such a manager would be! Too good to be true, he would be a man whose virtues were so daunting that all those in contact with him would be shamed. Such a person exists only in fiction; the truth is that imperfections and shortcomings, so long as they are known and disciplined by their possessor, make a manager the more real to those he is trying to manage. In other words, the manager must be a man, and no one would deny that mankind is imperfect.

Compassion, for example – the ability to understand with both head and heart the personal problems of the man or woman who comes for counsel: this is a quality that is compounded of humility and inner strength. Rarely does one meet cases of managers of high calibre who are not possessed of this gift of compassion to a high degree. When adjectives

like 'ruthless' or 'hard-hearted' or phrases like 'won't suffer
fools gladly' are applied to a manager it is pretty certain
that, however successful in the short term may be the operation he manages, in the long term no really sound edifice is
being built. The management atmosphere under these conditions is one of stress and strain, of shocks and uncertainties:
in a word, of insecurity. And it is this question of insecurity
which underlines so much of what is important to effective
management. The manager who can, by sheer force of
character and ability, diffuse a sense of ordered calm and
of planned progress is assured of a loyalty and esteem which
leaves far behind that race of obsequious 'anything for the
peace' characters who, seemingly inevitably, line up behind
the bullying autocrat to whom the word 'compassionate'
must sound naïve and unreal.

Having generalized in this way, we must examine in
greater detail some of the qualities that are sought in management. A proper assessment of at least some important
management qualities gives an opportunity to make a kind
of reckoning – to equate, so to say, the ideal and theoretical
with the practical, and to train the mind to a proper appreciation of much that is seldom appreciated. It is no alibi
merely to say that there are no golden rules.

*

A top-rating management quality is, of course, the ability to
think clearly. A muddled mind creates muddles around it.
Management is largely a question of decision, and decisions
cannot be properly taken unless the mind is clear about
objectives and priorities. To achieve that clarity of mind
calls for a form of concentration which is in itself a vital
discipline. Confused orders and delayed action are signs of
a management that is incapable of decisive thought.

It is generally true that the inability to think clearly stems
from an inadequate appreciation of what management

objectives and priorities are. A manager does not need to possess a huge intellect to do his job properly. What he needs far more urgently is a clear comprehension of what he is aiming at – the 'object of the exercise' – from which he is able to issue clear and unequivocal instructions because he is in no mental doubt about the purpose of his management task.

Once the objective is defined, it is remarkable how the 'thinking clearly' quality develops. Verbal or written instructions come forth loud and clear from the manager's lips or pen and, even if wrong actions or wrong decisions sometimes result, subordinates know where they stand. Bad decisions can often be better than no decisions at all.

It is perhaps the commonest complaint today of many just below management level that there is so much obscurity in the conveying of a manager's intentions. 'Tell us clearly what you want us to do and why you want us to do it, and we'll get on with it' is the plea of far too many who are the victims of the manager who is plainly unclear about what or why he is managing. Thinking it out is the only solution, and it should be education's highest object to train the mind to learn *how* to think.

*

In this technological age there are very few management tasks that do not call for a general understanding of technological operations. The questions are: how far should technical knowledge qualify for high management responsibility, and to what extent is the management function weakened (or perhaps enriched) by too much technical background?

These questions today form part of a great debate. The school of thought that presses for more and more technical know-how in management sees – and often with reason – considerable dangers to progress in the emergence of a purely management 'cadre'. They suspect the man or woman whose sole expertise is 'management' and who might obstruct a vital technical development because of an obsessive concern with, say, an organizational chart or a computer. There is also a school which says – and often with equal reason – that the very fact of the possession of technical knowledge in a high degree often eclipses imaginative thought and the 'human touch'. This school argues, often convincingly, that in a technological age the technocrat (that most unattractive of words) should not be taken out of the technical sphere, otherwise he will cause antagonisms and resentments. The very fact, it is argued, of considerable technical ability presupposes a mind closed to wider issues. The clinching argument produced by the first school – the 'management for management's sake' school – runs something like this: it says – and a mounting bibliography on management subjects would confirm this – that, in modern conditions, management needs its trained interpreters.

How true is the last argument? There is no question that management principles are beginning to emerge, and that the hit-or-miss methods of the old days will no longer do. The manager who says 'I don't know how I do it, but I do, and it seems to work successfully' has an aura of fustian about him. He may be right; it may well be that he has an instinctive feel for management and that he is unconcerned both with management techniques and technical know-how. He is, however, an exception from whom it would be wrong to try and prove a rule.

The danger would appear to lie more in the degree to which management itself becomes cocooned in its own technical know-how. The excessive self-consciousness about management which is a strong characteristic in industry and commerce today is surely an excellent thing, but it needs to be constantly reassessed; if the technicians in an industrial or commercial organization are to respect the work of trained management and accept that there is a place for it

– that, in fact, its existence is a guarantee of the recognition and progress of technological development – then it is essential that management should not be imprisoned in its own technology. It needs to beware of that single-mindedness which is, very often, the greatest strength of the technician.

In modern industrial conditions this is becoming a large problem. Top management needs a strong constitution to scale the heady slopes of technical development. Every day more and more questing scientists are being turned out who are dedicated to the improvement of a product or service. It is perhaps not so paradoxical as it may seem at first sight that, just as the technological pace accelerates, so do a host of other intangibles for management arise: 'modern' problems like communications within industry, public and labour relations, staff welfare, promotion, finance, dealings with shareholders – this is a small sample of the kind of things that need coping with, additionally to standard routines, in any progressive organization. How can it be possible for a man or woman who has reached a high point of technological experience, and whose mind is reaching for more and more such experience, to deal with these more ephemeral, but equally important, management aspects?

Maybe the true answer to the conundrum lies somewhere between both schools of thought. What is probably needed today more than ever is the manager whose technical know-how stops short of detail and who has, at a point in his or her career, opted for the wider horizons. One thing is certain: the manager must keep abreast, so far as he is able, of the technical aspects of the merchandise or services, or both, for which he is responsible. Anxiously determined to appear infallible, many a manager will give an impression of comprehension simply because he hasn't the moral courage to admit otherwise. The technical people are thus confused and confounded. A basic understanding of the problem under discussion is, under present exacting technological conditions, of great importance, if only to avoid being 'blinded by science' and to be spared the private scorn of a subordinate who knows that his superior is completely baffled by the technical arguments put forward.

*

This last point leads almost naturally into the question of integrity in management. True integrity lies precisely in the ability to admit when one *is* fogged, when the issue is *not* clear, when, with the best will in the world, a subordinate's argument is simply *not* understood. Nothing is more likely to undermine the prestige of a manager than the discovery that he is bluffing. This is far more serious, in relation to the handling of subordinates, than a frank admission of defeat or ignorance or a plain 'don't know'. The old concept of a leader who 'knows all and sees all' is a dying one. The pace of modern life simply does not admit of the existence of the kind of Nietzschean figure, august and Olympian, a master mind before whom lesser beings make their obeisance. It is possibly only among the teachers of today that one finds something of that detachment which comes from wide knowledge. The manager cannot afford the luxury of too much detachment; he must have an integrity which admits his imperfections, so that from those imperfections he will be the better placed to understand the weaknesses of those he has been called upon to manage.

Integrity is often defined as honesty, but it can also mean 'wholeness'. To be complete in oneself – not perfect but complete – assures the transmission of a very special quality to others. This completeness is a paramount gift to a manager. There are echoes here of Jan Christian Smuts, with his study 'Holism and Evolution'. Smuts believed that 'every individual form of life is a unity, a centre of activity dominated by one fundamental property. It is this ultimate internal unity that shapes the innumerable products of life into an orderly and harmonious whole.' His idea of Holism as an attempt at synthesis – an 'attempt at bringing together any currents of thought and development' – is apt. It suggests that the whole is greater than the sum of its parts, and it is just in this wholeness of outlook that the manager can uniquely contribute to the welding together of the hopes and fears of all those he is managing.

How is he to achieve this integrity, this wholeness?

It is surely a manager's task, in the well-worn cliché, to 'explore every avenue'. Everything should be of excitement and interest to him. Prejudice, preconceptions, dogma, and bigotry should be anathema. He should strive all the time to ripen his mind by reading as many books, seeing as many plays, pictures, and films, listening to as much music, and talking to as many people as time will allow. And this attractive catalogue of activity does not include travel, hobbies, family life, and all the rest. These too, have immense value in producing a mind that is flexible and absorbent. It is not always so easy for the manager to get these opportunities to broaden his mind. It is a particular form of self-discipline, necessary to the achievement of 'wholeness', that he should force himself to rise above the routines of his job. A timely book might be written which would examine the effects of television on the tired manager who deludes himself that the vicarious information and entertainment television supplies is of enduring value to him. It is surely the personal and private mental adventure, the journey down what Francis Thompson called 'the labyrinthine ways' of his own mind, that makes for completeness of outlook.

It is far from easy under present-day conditions to achieve that relaxed quality which seems to be a part of the man or woman who has learned at the appropriate moment how to put his or her management problems, however large or trivial, aside. The competiveness of life, the press of events, and the mass of information that is poured forth from press, television, and radio conspire to eliminate private thinking. These outside influences seem to strike at the very root of individual effort and enterprise. 'We'll think for you' they seem to say. And, equally, the stream of textbooks that grows with every year suggests to the lazy mind that 'it's all down in writing – you only have to know where to look for it'.

It is a very special aspect of this matter of the quality of integrity that the manager should bring original thinking to the management task. How can the thinking be truly original if the thinker operates with second-hand or borrowed thoughts?

Of the 'honesty' aspect of integrity in a manager it is hardly necessary to write at length. The manager who is in any way suspect is doomed. There is, it is true, a sadly topical angle to this subject. With the growth of taxation and controls, in fact in the complex conditions of trading today, a great deal of time has to be spent fighting battles with the authorities. This is a commentary on our times and the battle is unlikely to decrease in tempo. What should a manager who rates integrity high do about this situation? How far should he compromise his high standards?

He would be an imprudent man who attempted easy answers to these questions. On balance, it is clearly better to respect regulations, reserving always the right to fight them rather than cheat when there are anomalies and injustices. There is no very great respect from lower down for a manager who is known to be defrauding the authorities, however iniquitous the law may be. This aspect of management integrity is very much in the forefront today. While there might be momentary admiration, for example, for a manager who has twisted the Revenue's tail, it is doubtful whether, in the long term, that the same manager will be entirely trusted by his own people.

However limited, or large, the management sphere may be, this surely applies. The 'wide boy', be he a foreman or a chairman, is an unattractive, untrustworthy figure. Honesty in the sense used here is truth, and with truth there is no compromise.

In the last analysis, the job of the manager is to retain the confidence of those he is managing. Without such confidence his authority is dissipated.

*

It is important not to confuse sharp practices with acumen and enterprise. The resourceful manager can deploy his resourcefulness without compromising his standards. This is easy to say, but it constitutes a considerable challenge to management; it often seems so much simpler to achieve a certain end by the adroit use of questionable methods. A recurring example is in the field of staff relations. A manager will sometimes go to tortuous lengths to avoid speaking frankly and fearlessly to a subordinate about a fault. With acumen, i.e. choosing the psychological moment, and enterprise, i.e. finding an original, not too wounding, way to communicate, a rapidly deteriorating staff situation can be saved. To try to find less straightforward ways of telling a man where he stands, to employ a third party, or to trump up some irrelevant device is the opposite of good management.

In a wider context, acumen and enterprise are management qualities of great worth. Are they instinctive gifts or can they be learnt? Are they the result of hard-won experience? Can they stand by themselves? Are they complementary?

Answering the first two questions together, it would seem that these are qualities that are innate, but that they can both be developed with education and experience. It is doubtful whether true acumen – the ability shrewdly and penetratingly to assess a situation – can be developed by someone not born with an instinctive discernment and sense of discrimination. The development of this instinctive sense can be partly self-taught and partly learnt from example. Enterprise is a somewhat different quality. Stamina and luck enter into it. The enterprising man, it will often be noticed in industry, is the man whose adventurous and experimental spirit has met up with a cautious, prudent foil (often a deputy or assistant) who helps to turn an idea into practical politics. The entrepreneur makes the millions and the foil remains – a foil. But enterprise in management can, of course, be much more than that: it can mean courage, flair and foresight. It can mean the possession of the 'inner eye', that priceless gift of being just a jump ahead of what people are thinking and wanting and doing.

Enterprise and acumen are not enough by themselves. They are complementary qualities in management, but they are not the whole story. The plans of the shrewdest, most audacious manager can founder on the rocks of maladroit handling of people, of lack of basic integrity.

*

Earlier in this chapter we spoke of 'the manager who can by sheer force of character and ability, diffuse a sense of ordered calm and planned progress.' This diffusion process is largely a matter of communications. In enumerating management 'qualities' the power to communicate must rate very high. There are far too many managers who are secretive about their intentions and who feel that there is some sort of loss of dignity or 'face' – or even power – in making sure that, all down the line, everyone knows what they are about. In later chapters some practical illustrations of how this can be done will be discussed. At this point, when the often intangible qualities to be sought for in a manager are under review, the quality of mind that can see a management task as a great deal more than issuing orders, that can, in fact, help towards creating an atmosphere of mutual goodwill based on knowledge of what is going on, is a quality of high importance. Much is being said and written these days about the workers' interest, or lack of interest, in management objectives. It is fashionable in an 'I'm all right Jack' mood to pooh-pooh any suggestion that, in fact, workers genuinely care for what the operation by which they are employed is trying to achieve, and it is, of course, easy to be cynical or sentimental about this most crucial of issues. The ability to communicate is a key to the problem – not just the ability to think clearly and pass clear thoughts down the line, but to work out a communications plan which takes care of the character and the ramifications of the group to be communicated to. It is better to tell too much than not enough. This particular quality is another of the instinctive ones. There are many managers who lack the imagination, the instinct, to realize that what they are doing is of infinite interest to others. They feel a sense of constraint, as if shouting the odds were somehow not quite in the best of taste.

Equally it is a considerable management quality to know when and how to communicate, and to whom. A manager who announces a new contract before it is finally clinched, or a foreman who in a nose-tapping mood discloses wage increases before they have been agreed, can turn communications into a nonsense. Nevertheless, if one takes the highest common factor of all that is said and written about management qualities, the question of communications is high on the list. In the admirable 'Proceedings' of H.R.H. the Duke of Edinburgh's first Study Conference the theme throughout was the question of keeping in touch – not just 'togetherness' in the somewhat mushy context in which the word is used today, but the achievement of wholeness through sharing.

*

Humanity and intelligence as management qualities are indivisible and add up to a fine formula for leadership. *Intelligence* that is not necessarily of an intellectual kind, but that is the sum total of the qualities discussed in previous sections of this chapter, guarantees a humane outlook because it is, of itself, intensely human. The manager, manifestly strong in some respects, weak in others, but intelligent enough to understand himself, is a good leader; Intelligence should not mean arrogance or superiority; humanity should not mean weakness or sentimentality.

It is sometimes argued that the best manager is just the ordinary chap, the average man who is no better and no worse than the next one, the man who has plodded along to responsibility and power. Too often are quoted (and usually incorrectly) adaptations of the famous remark 'every French soldier carries in his cartridge-pouch the baton of a marshal of France', and too often it is forgotten that these words were Napoleon's – a convenient generalization for a genius to propound. Is management responsibility – no matter how great or small the area over which it has to be exercised – in fact something calling for qualities of leadership which, in the final reckoning, are inborn? Are such qualities intuitive rather than assimilable?

The phrase 'a natural leader' is one answer to the question. Leadership *is* a natural function to some and totally unnatural to others. In an increasingly complicated world more and more people want to be led rather than to lead. Fear of life and life's purposes produces mass religious and political followings which, lulled by the narcotic of authoritarian manoeuvre, tend to place more and more power into the hands of less and less people. This is an ironic and tragic negation of the democratic ideal but it is an unmistakable trend of our times. This situation puts the problem of management leadership in a democratic community in a searching light. Can the 'natural leaders' be found, encouraged, and be given sufficient outlet for their talents so as to prevent such talents being diverted to destructive and empty causes? Does the growing characteristic of mankind to move in a mass and to live vicariously mean that leadership for good rather than bad reasons will flourish or wither?

In any consideration of management leadership, thought must be given to a quality about which it is hard to write in precise terms: that of enthusiasm. If it is true to say that a cynical approach to management problems is a possible consequence of the uncertainties of these times, enthusiasm becomes a rare and precious commodity, which communicates itself very quickly to those who are managed. Of course, enthusiasm by itself is not enough, but the manager who can combine intelligence and humanity with a genuine enthusiasm is likely to be a true leader. In this respect management in Great Britain needs to do some new thinking. There is something faintly scornful in the national attitude to enthusiasm. Inherent shyness, an almost pathological dislike of flamboyance or 'showing off', suspicion of emotional rather than controlled attitudes – whatever it may be, the British, wedded to understatement, tend to take a jaundiced view of the enthusiast. And this has often resulted in a serious loss to the community of leaders of great potential merit who, dispirited and discouraged by a nebulous yet discernible hostility to their enthusiasm, give up the unequal struggle and join the growing ranks of managers-who-might-have-been.

*

It was suggested at the start of this chapter that there are no golden rules governing the qualities of management. The contrariness and contradictions of human nature make this so. There are many cases of men and women effectively carrying management responsibilities today who are totally lacking in the qualities under discussion but who command loyalty through some personal quality which is incapable of analysis – an emanation of almost psychic character which hynotizes subordinates into unquestioning devotion. Equally there are thousands of managers who, working from a foundation of innate gifts, painstakingly study management principles but never make the leadership grade.

Neither of these contrary situations excuses the need to think hard about those qualities which make for good management. Whether we like it or not, modern society cannot keep going without organization and organization calls for sound and enlightened leadership. From the vast trading organization via the galaxy of small businesses, professional undertakings, and government agencies, down to the family unit itself there must be managers and managed, and the absence of a golden rule makes the management task the more exciting. Anyone who has had the good fortune to have worked under a man or woman of high management quality will recognize a very special human experience; and there are, perhaps surprisingly, many men and women today of middle age who think back wistfully to some of their commanders in the war. It is an irony that the challenge of emergency and crisis should be needed to bring out powers of leadership.

A great deal of everyone's time is spent either managing or being managed. How essential it is, then, in this new industrial revolution – the revolution which is throwing up not only a mass of new and ingenious management aids and techniques but the manager himself as the key figure in the organizational scheme of things – that qualities of management, elusive and tenuous though they may be, should be under ceaseless examination.

When all is said and done, the one management quality that is inborn and that is, in its way, priceless is that of character. This book will show – it will certainly try to – that a manager's job can be analysed in reasonably scientific detail and that with training and experience much of it can be learnt. But the possession of character illumines the whole process. It adds to competence a lustre which is of unique value because it opens up vistas, denied to so many, of courage, imagination, and adventure.

3

Management or Leadership – or Both?

MOST discussions about management start off with a search
for the best definition of the word. The truth is that the
management function is so subtle, its applications so diverse,
and its interpretations and interpreters so varied that there
are no ready-made answers. It is for this reason that in this
book qualities of management are discussed in an early
chapter, for it is from a consideration of these qualities that
the first inkling of what management really is appears. Consider, for example, the definition in the *Concise Oxford
Dictionary* of the verb 'to manage'. This can vary in meaning from 'to handle, wield control', via 'to contrive' (ironically) in the sense of 'he managed to make a muddle', 'to
succeed in one's aim' or 'to make proper use of'. And the
word 'management'. The dictionary quite bluntly says that
its meaning can range from the 'art of handling' to the
business of 'deceitful contrivance'. No wonder no very
durable definitions have emerged so far from the many and
laudable attempts that have been made to answer this tricky
question!

And yet the dictionary definitions – wide as they may be
in meaning – relate very clearly to the behaviour of man
himself. The implication surely is that management depends
to a large degree on the type of person who is doing the
managing – the controller, the handler, the contriver, even
the muddler. This in turn must condition the 'management'
definition. If it is accepted that management is one of the
most active and the least passive of human occupations
then there was certainly nothing illogical in considering
what qualities should be sought for in a manager before

feeling towards the solution of what management really is.

It is often said that management is the day-to-day control by the full-time directors of a business as well as by those immediately below them who are responsible to the Board. The standards of the business and its pattern are said to derive from these stimuli.

This is an over-simplification. The changing pattern of business has completely altered what might be called an oligarchical concept of business management. It is true that full-time directors and their immediate subordinates should work out policy and objectives, but for a business operation to succeed the management process must be repeated all the way down the line. A supervisor is every bit as much a manager as a director, for however high the standard may be that is set by the top direction, however clear the patterns that are laid down, the whole process can founder if there is a weak link in the chain. Obvious examples are the cases of manufacturers whose poor labour relations upset the most carefully thought-out merchandising policies, or a nationalized industry in which Board directions become dulled by the frustrations and intrigues of those whose job it is to carry them out.

If it is accepted that management is a continuous process and that an effectively managed undertaking is one in which, from top to bottom, there is a clear understanding of management aims by people able to grasp and interpret them, the search for definitions becomes less obscure. Management cannot be separated from leadership. This is not to say that management *is* leadership, for that would be another over-simplification; but it at least indicates that for those trying to determine the nature of management, pure management, although a science, a technique, needs to be buttressed by leadership – and leadership is a mixture of art, craft, and humanity.

Let us express this thought in another way. Management

today is responsive to a great number of techniques which take away many of the hazards. As suitable an example as any is that of work study. The worst miscalculations in the laying down of wage scales can be avoided, in many instances, if an analytical study of working methods is undertaken which takes proper cognizance of the true nature of the task. These principles are now almost a truism and have a wide acceptance throughout industry and commerce. Or market research. Much of the guesswork can be taken out of the evolution of a marketing policy if market research properly planned and interpreted, is used to help chart a course. Or budgeting. Management is leaning more and more on clearly defined systems of controls – production, sales, and financial – in order to eliminate the hit-or-miss atmosphere in which many businesses are conducted. These are three random examples of techniques which contribute toward the creation of a form of management which may fairly be described as scientific. They are, so to say, 'musts' in conditions of competition, and desirable in any situation, competitive or otherwise. Each technique, in given circumstances, is invaluable to managers who want to know exactly where a business is going and how it is likely to fare on the way.

But neither work study, nor market research, nor budgetary control is of value in itself if the leadership element is lacking. Work study must be carried out in a cooperative receptive atmosphere; market research can only supply facts and is no substitute for dynamic marketing; budgetary controls are worthless if those who are expected to work them are not seized with their value. That an atmosphere should be receptive to a new technique, that a fundamental business operation should be dynamic, and that profit controls should be worked intelligently call for a 'climate' in a business that only leadership can achieve.

It is, however, important not to confuse management

techniques with the art of leadership. The two are complementary but they are not the same thing. Techniques which are being developed daily as business pressures rise are being studied by more and more people who are becoming specialists in them. The leadership element, however, is constant: it is an art that is timeless. There are no such people as leadership specialists, and anyone laying claim to such knowledge should be highly suspect.

Granted that management is a science and leadership an art there is still the unsolved question of how these two functions should be fused to ensure the best of all worlds. If management is arid without leadership and leadership purposeless without management, can the discussion be taken a stage further by considering the difference – and, indeed, deciding if there *is* a difference – between the descriptions 'a well-managed business' and 'a well-led business'?

A well-managed business does not necessarily contain within it the seeds of progress. The organization may be perfect, the methods impeccable, the conditions ideal; but without that extra something, so hard to define yet so potent, today's success might quickly turn into tomorrow's failure. This is surely because sound management, being scientific, lacks the 'plus' quality which only leadership can produce. A good analogy can be taken from the Army – it is the contrast between the 'Q' branch and the Command. The 'Q' branch ensures the smooth efficient flow of the operation, but without inspired command the battle would never be won.

*

There is a recurring example which deserves detailed comment at this point. This is the matter of recognition, either by status or pay, of services rendered. Too often good men and women are lost to an organization because of a manager's realization, too late, of their qualities – too late in the sense that another post has offered itself and the damage has been done. Management can, and often does, work out admirable salary and wages scales which are based on unexceptionable calculations and which take into consideration every sort of work factor. But, often, these scales involve a rigidity which takes no note of the exceptional circumstance or man; which, in fact, lacks the human touch. Case histories of poor business management are full of examples of able men and women attracted away to other companies simply because the initiative in keeping such people under the eye of the direction, in making them feel that they are getting encouragement, is not kept by the management itself. Over and over again stories are to be heard of executives in lower echelons who, announcing to their seniors that they have decided to go elsewhere, are then suddenly appreciated and cajoled to remain with promises of more money and status. This is poverty of leadership. There should be ceaseless review, at all levels, of the human material at management's disposal and the review can only be effectively made by those with leadership flair – with what the opening chapter called the 'inner eye'. Such attention to 'talent spotting' is not a form of favouritism. It does not presuppose that good business leaders will indulge in capricious selection. It does, however, suggest that, while in every working community there will be a vast proportion who want to be told what do do and be left to get on with it, it is the minority that needs succour and encouragement – those who want to put more into their jobs and get more out of them.

Neat management can look after ninety-nine per cent of the problem but leadership makes sure that the remaining one per cent, which may be crucial, is not moulded into the routine pattern. A well-led business fully understands how to use and deploy management techniques. It is in the process of 'full understanding' that leadership emerges.

*

It is important not to get leadership out of proportion. Leadership alone is not enough. In the conditions of industry, trade, and finance leadership derives tremendously from the backing of really efficient management – it is, indeed, sustained by it. That most controversial of figures, Lord Montgomery, would not deny that his desert success was a striking blend of leadership and management; he saw most clearly that all the inspiration in the world would not beat Rommel if it were not supported by the cold facts of efficient management at every level below him, extending to the fighting soldier himself. The world is, however, full of leaders in a vacuum: men and women of great flair and enthusiasm who, lacking the ability or the resources to translate their leadership into action become embittered and defeatist.

Fine words on this subject of leadership, which of its very nature must be somewhat speculative, come from another soldier, Lord Slim, who, when lecturing some years ago in Australia to the Australian Institute of Management said:

There is a difference between leadership and management. The leader and the men who follow him represent one of the oldest, most natural and most effective of all human relationships. The manager and those he manages are a later product, with neither so romantic nor so inspiring a history. Leadership is of the spirit, compounded of personality and vision; its practice is an art. Management is of the mind, more a matter of accurate calculation, of statistics, of methods, timetables and routine; its practice is a science. Managers are necessary; leaders are essential.

*

For the rest of this book the word management will be used in its widest sense and will assume that the leadership element is not lacking. Enough has been said to demonstrate that the manager, to be truly effective, must either be well led or possess the qualities of a leader. As the argument

develops much space will have to be given, and rightly, to
those aspects of management which have a considerable
scientific content in them. It will be proper to consider in
detail, for example, how the best possible use can be made of
men, materials, and methods – a vital management factor.
Dominating such examinations, which will point, helpfully
it is hoped, to 'scientific' aids in each case, must be the basic
human problem. However scientifically an 'end' is planned,
the 'means' must take note of human strength and frailty.
Perhaps it is at this point that one can discern a fundamental difference between a free and an unfree way of life.
The free way of life, for all its shortcomings and retrogres-
sions, tries to recognize, as it marches towards a higher
standard of living for an ever greater number, the essential
dignity of the individual. The unfree way of life is con-
temptuous of such thinking: the individual counts for little
in the wider concept of the State.

It is not the present purpose to enter the complicated
realms of politics and metaphysics, but it is the clear duty of
anyone who is trying to express management objectives to
set the question against a wider, ideological background.
The security of free peoples is being challenged daily by the
growth of power among those whose management methods
may be highly scientific but who take little or no cognizance
of human values. Leadership in management in the western
world must therefore gear itself to deal realistically with the
problem it faces and equate a consideration for people's
feelings with the size of the challenge. It is easy enough to
write this, but how formidable a question it is can only be
measured by realizing that the race is on and that it is going
to be a hard one to win. In the matter of nuclear development, for example, Russia and China can deploy resources
of manpower which leave the democracies standing. What
is the democratic leader to do? How far can he compromise
his principles with expediency?

The West is by no means clear of those business organizations which still cling anachronistically to the idea that 'men are expendable'. But time is not on their side – neither time nor the aggregate social conscience. What was good enough in the late eighteenth or nineteenth centuries of ruthless and rapid industrialization is no longer acceptable today. It is at this point that leadership and management are completely fused. Good management must concern itself with getting the maximum possible from the managed: good leadership must see to it that this maximum is achieved in harmony and understanding.

It is the quintessence of leadership in management to be able to secure cooperation all along the line in both palatable and unpalatable tasks. When the cooperation calls for a degree of self-sacrifice, this can be achieved only by a fearless statement by management of what is at stake. It is surely not possible to discover what such issues might be until there is a clearer understanding of *how* one manages, *what* one is managing, and for *whom*.

4

The Business of Management

MANAGEMENT stems from leadership. This book will already have failed in its purpose if it has not made that clear. Whatever systems, whatever mechanics, whatever charts are worked out for the more efficient prosecution of a business, top management must be convinced about what it wants to do and must be able to explain its convictions to all those who are part of the operation – of whatever size. This ability to communicate a desired 'end' – whether the communicator is the chairman of a Board speaking for a company employing thousands, or a small shopkeeper taking on his first assistant, or a foreman calling for a special effort – must be the priority in the actual matter of managing. Enough has been written already, it is hoped, to demonstrate that the factors making for that kind of management leadership are intangible and largely 'human'. In essence it is the will of the manager which must be communicated inspiringly.

Nevertheless the inexorable conditions of modern business – competition, the growing desire for more leisure, and the belated recognition of the need for 'a fair day's wages for a day worked' – mean that there is a great deal more to management than stating an aim and hoping to achieve it. Personality alone – even if it is backed by inspired leadership coupled with clear statements of what is expected – will not run a business profitably. While it is true that there are no absolute rights or absolute wrongs in the evolution of principles of organization, there are some basic organizational truths which need to be recognized and discussed. To suggest, as some management experts suggest, that there are, in fact, forms of organization that are one-hundred-per-cent correct, copybook organizations so to speak, is surely both unreal and arrogant. Personalities and problems change with the passing of time. There is no one solution, organizationally, to managing a man or a body of men; but that is no excuse for doing nothing and depending on some remote power to make sure that it will all come right in the end.

The present concern is with the question 'how does a manager manage?' It must be stated right at the start that it is impossible for management to escape from the responsibility of sitting down and evolving some organizational procedures. This is crucial. Are there, in fact, any general considerations about organization and the preparation of an organizational structure which can be set out as being firm and reliable? And what does the word organization mean? Taking the second question first, organization is the process of identifying and grouping activities for the most effective achievement of the policy of an undertaking. The duties and responsibilities of the various groups and individuals need to be carefully defined and the most suitable executive and procedural framework (such as clearly expressed standing instructions) drawn up to fit the special conditions of each company. Portentous words, perhaps, but they are at the heart of the matter.

If the point is accepted that a business's profitability and its capacity to develop successfully in the interests of everybody in it are the two essential business purposes, then much will depend on the effectiveness of the organization's structure as well as the ability of its executives. It is essential to plan what the functions, as laid down in the organization structure, need to be and how they should be best grouped to achieve effective management. It is only then that a clear idea emerges of the qualities and experience that must be demanded from the various executives charged with filling the posts so evolved. It is only at that point that the expressions 'Planning for Growth' or 'Long-range Planning' make any kind of sense.

The primary responsibility is that of the Board, or the working proprietors, or any equivalent top management group. These are the people who must determine the policy and the objectives of a company, while representing the interests of, and accepting a great sense of responsibility to, all concerned in the enterprise. Above all, and too often neglected as a top management responsibility, the Board must provide the judgement and guidance for the correct organization and control of the enterprise so as to ensure that the objectives are attained.

A point should be made here about part-time directors. In this age of specialization there is often much to be said for the introduction into a company's top counsels of men or women who can give competent and objective advice on particular management aspects. Such people are able to produce a detached view which is in no way troubled by the internal politics, the intrigues, of the enterprise they are advising. They can be immensely helpful over problems such as industrial relations, finance, and marketing, and they are particularly valuable to the smaller business in which the directors tend to be far too close to management problems. What they cannot do is to replace the essential contact with executives which the day-to-day senior management must maintain. There are considerable differences in the approach to this question. Insurance companies and banks, in Britain at least, tend to people their Boards with a great number of distinguished names and, except in rare instances, do not put the chief executive on the Board. There is also an infinity of smaller businesses which looks askance at the idea of anyone sharing in policy decisions who has not, so to speak, worked his passage. Vast organizations like I.C.I. or Unilever appear to believe in a mixture of the two. The recently created motor vehicle giant, British Leyland Motor

Corporation Ltd., takes the view that only very few part-timers are necessary. The American approach is to have a majority of non-executive directors allegedly representing the public and keeping the 'irresponsible' executives under control.

It should also be emphasized, while writing of Board responsibility, that the same principles apply whatever size the operation may be. It is just as important for the shop-keeper mentioned at the start of this chapter to plan what he wants his new assistant to do and why – and to explain his wants in clear unmistakable terms – as it is for the fore-man and supervisor to think out in detail the organization for the special effort his superior management has asked him and his colleagues to make. The Board must be the main policy maker because, in fact, policy has to come from the top – policy, objectives, and leadership.

It is necessary here to inject a truism. Top management must bear the responsibility for working out objectives, but the building of the organization to achieve those objectives is not an end in itself. It is simply the means to an end. It is the successful pursuit of the objectives that is truly the end. The finest organization brains and money can devise will never produce the desired result if the end is obscure. Pre-occupation with organizational problems has tended to be-devil many enterprises in which, had the objectives, the ends, been crystal clear, the means of achieving them would have fallen quickly and logically into place. The case studies in failure at the end of this book will vividly demonstrate this point.

But what is meant by objectives? It is becoming increas-ingly clear to business management that subordinates can-not be expected to take particularly serious objectives that are put forward to them in broad, windy phrases. The objective must be easy to assimilate, reasonable of achieve-ment; it must carry with it the ring of conviction, but if it is evangelical it will be highly suspect. That very great man Field-Marshal Earl Wavell in his *Soldiers and Soldiering* says of Cromwell's Ironsides that 'they knew what they were fighting for and loved what they knew'. Many, possibly cynical, managers today would say that this is highly irrelevant in modern conditions when causes and objectives are overshadowed by purely material considerations. It is one thing to know what the objectives are: to hope that they will be universally approved is quite another matter. And so the leadership element in management again appears, for to make the objective intelligible and worthwhile is, in the last resort, a leader's task. One more quotation used by Lord Wavell and which comes from a book about the Second World War, will suffice:

A man does not flee because he is fighting in an unrighteous cause. He does not attack because his cause is just. He flees because he is the weaker; he conquers because he is the stronger or because his leader has made him feel the stronger. . . .

*

It has been said earlier in this chapter that there must be caution in the matter of laying down organizational rules. Size, function, and location are but three of many determining factors in this matter. Some rules are better than none at all, and it may be a useful guide at this point to take an average-sized industrial operation employing, say, several thousand people. Management theorists have spent much time considering the expedients that should be followed in considering the soundness of such an organization. Seven rules – if the word rules must be used – are here suggested:

1. There must be a clear definition of executive duties and responsibilities.
2. Each branch, department, or section, should have one main duty.

3. Each branch, department, or section should be an entity under the control of one executive.

4. The number of subordinates responsible to one executive should normally be between five and eight except in special circumstances.

5. The grouping of secondary responsibilities should be dependent on the capabilities of the personnel available and their duties should be clearly defined.

6. Distinction should be made between direct executive and functional responsibilities, and the methods of communication for functional specialists must be clearly laid down.

7. There should be the maximum delegation of operational responsibility with adequate safeguards for management control.

Organization needs to be thought about with a very open mind. If the above seven 'rules' are used as a check list, it is suggested that a useful structural framework will often emerge.

*

New words are appearing in this chapter – new words, that is to say, in the context of organization for management – such as 'delegation', 'control', and 'communication'. These have a considerable bearing on the question of how a manager manages and must be considered in some detail. What do management theorists actually mean when they talk of 'maximum delegation'?

The principle here is clear. Delegation implies trust. There are a number of factors that influence the extent to which delegation is either possible or desirable. A major task of anyone managing is to take decisions, and as management becomes more technical and more complex, more and more decisions have to be made. Furthermore, if one accepts that there is a limit to the number of people an executive can deal with, so to speak, executively, it is essential that decisions should be shared. Though possibly an over-simplification, it may be said that there are two sorts of decision: policy decision and crisis decision; and it also follows that decisions (this word is appearing a great deal, but is highly relevant to this chapter) vary in the way they commit an undertaking in the future and in the number of people they affect. As production, marketing, and financial techniques improve, policy decisions become increasingly separated from crisis decisions, because a greater number of rational factors enter into the decision-making process. Management, in a word, becomes analytical and less intuitive.

An example here will make the point clearer. Let it be assumed that a middle-sized firm with two plants is run by an executive board which contains a managing director, sales, works, and design directors, and the company secretary. The top organization might well look like this:

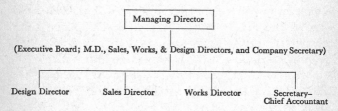

Objectives of company policy are hammered out by the Executive Board which, in the event of some major decision, may consult the fuller Board, which might have on it some part-time members. These executives, so far as they are able, should keep themselves clear of detail. They should be concerned with policy rather than crisis. They should, above all, work as a team. It has become clear that a small, closely knit, mutually trusting group is most likely to provide the right kind of policy-making, objective-setting leadership. It is almost a law of nature that one or two members of such a team will emerge as the leaders, the men or women who through sheer force of character and ability are turned to by the others for the final judgement, but in general the conception of the dominating Number One is slowly dying. The complexity of management, the range of knowledge required, make this so. Examination of the top structure of most successful businesses will show how this team concept is replacing the former idea of the all-powerful chief executive, usually surrounded by second-rate, sycophantic nonentities. Such a man, in today's management conditions, needs to be three people: he has to combine benevolence (courtesy to workers at staff parties and a pleasant personality with shareholders and the press) with dynamism (the zestful energy, optimism, resilience and restless curiosity of the man of action) and with erudition (the ability to think deeply, to plan ahead, to take a philosophical, detached view of his task). Such a man hardly ever exists. Plato wrote of balancing temperaments and that is precisely what a top executive group needs today. The real problem is the mammoth company in which the top management team inevitably becomes more and more removed from the day-to-day 'feel' of the operation and its stresses and strains, while it expends much energy in the struggle for the succession. Some years ago it was revealed by a study undertaken in the U.S.A. that some of the best-run large businesses are those in which the salary levels of the top executives are much the same, so that there is not that dizzy height of financial reward to scale if any one of the top few wants to reach the summit. There must be much to be said for the team whose standard of living is broadly parallel: when the managing director occupies a stately home and the other directors service flats, there are bound to be disturbing tensions! Vance Packard's books, *The Pyramid Climbers* and *The Status Seekers*, make diverting and instructive reading in this connexion. As organizations in Britain get larger and larger the parallel with the U.S.A. (Packard's area of research) gets even closer.

Given, then, that a sound top management team is in charge of the two-plant operation under discussion, how does the Works Director, for example, make sure that crises are coped with so that every minute of his day, when his mind should be thinking outwards rather than inwards, is usefully filled? An organization that suggests itself in this instance would look like this:

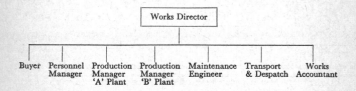

If the Works Director has sufficient faith in the quality of the seven men he has selected for these key delegated jobs, he will leave the crises to them. A typical imaginary situation might be the following. The sequence of operations in the processing of a product involves nickel plating as a final process. An unanticipated breakdown in the electrical controls of 'B' plant puts this vital equipment out of action for a period of a minimum of two or three days. In order that an important production batch should not be interrupted, the Production Manager of 'B' plant decides, after consultation with his Maintenance Engineer, to see whether the process can be met by an outside sub-contractor. This is organized, and not only is the work done to a standard higher than anything which the Company itself has been able previously to achieve, but also the process time is shorter and the works Accountant reports that the cost was lower than the Company's own normal process cost.

This was a crisis decision which has – quite rightly – been dealt with by the Production Manager within his delegated sphere of authority. The Works Director, in any case, was away in Western Europe with the Managing Director, looking into certain implications of the Common Market, in connexion with overseas manufacturing. On his return, the crisis being resolved, questions of policy arise. Is it right for the Company to retain its plating plant (which in any case is only a process and not part of the main manufacturing plant) when outside sub-contractors can meet their requirement more quickly, more cheaply, and more effectively? Is future design policy likely to lead to more or less high-finish plating? Will the size of future products (which affects plating tanks particularly) be likely to vary? If the Company's own small plating shop is to be eliminated altogether, what would happen to the work-people and could they be absorbed elsewhere? What negotiations would be necessary? Is the space so released suitable for badly-needed expansion? The list is a formidable one and only a few sample problems are put down. These are policy matters which arise from a crisis – a crisis which only delegated and trusted authority could solve at once.

The foregoing must not be taken to suggest that management is delegated purely to cope with crises. In the normal running of a business there are as many routine as there are crisis decisions. The crisis point is simply emphasized to underline the fact that a top management should not allow itself to go off at tangents. Immediate problems are more appropriately handled by men on the spot who should have the assurance which truly delegated authority confers. A senior executive should have an empty desk and an open mind.

*

'Rule' four suggested that the number of subordinates responsible to one executive should normally not exceed eight except in special circumstances. The question of the span of control must depend to a great extent on the personalities involved and the technical nature of the operation. There are certain types of manager whose energy is prodigious and whose appetite for work voracious. To limit such men and women to controlling a fixed number of people would be foolish; equally, there are so many highly technical management operations involving much thought, time, and talk that it would be impossible for a manager, in these conditions, to do justice to the control of more than a minimum of subordinates. In any case personality is an overriding factor. There are businesses today which still depend to an overwhelming extent on the drive and enthusiasm of one man or woman. To shackle drive and enthusiasm to the perfections of a settled span of control – however well it might look on paper and however logical it might sound organizationally – would be sacrificing very special advantages.

There is however a clear distinction between a 'span of control', subject as it is to the kind of limitations and qualifications discussed in the previous paragraph, and the far more important question of managerial responsibility. It may well be, for example, that in the branch office of a shipping company the manager can only do justice, in terms of control, to a handful of people but this must surely not be confused with his responsibilities which extend to the most recently joined member of the staff and which need to recognize the potential of every single human being in his charge. There is a world of difference between managing and controlling people; management implies the development of everyone's talents around the manager. Control is a straightforward organizational matter. There is a useful passage in Peter Drucker's *Practice of Management* which merits full quotation here:

The span of control, we are told, cannot exceed six or eight subordinates. The span of managerial responsibility, however, is determined by the extent to which assistance and teaching are needed. It can only be set by a study of the concrete situation. Unlike the span of control, the span of managerial responsibility broadens as we move upwards in the organization. . . . The span of managerial responsibility is therefore wider than the span of control and where good practice would counsel against stretching the span of control, a manager should always have responsibility for a few more men than he can really take care of. Otherwise the temptation is to supervise them, that is, to take over their jobs or, at least, to breathe down their necks. . . .

And it is here, when using the word control, that we meet, head-on, the first great development in management techniques over the last ten years – that of the proper organization and use of systems developed to provide a flow of management information. Control need no longer be a compound of hunch and experience and leadership. It can be underpinned by an accurate feed-back, scientifically collected and interpreted, which eliminates a lot of the guesswork from the control process.

*

Delegation must not be confused with decentralization. Delegation is a question of trust and expediency; the need for decentralization arises from growth. It is primarily an organizational matter.

When an organization grows in size a point is reached when it can be far more effectively managed by regrouping the functions so as to give local managers greater responsibility. For example, a new factory may be set up to manufacture a complete set of products. Initially it may be that the manager is only concerned with production, but later he may have added factory accountancy, research, and sales to his responsibilities. Or banking and insurance. These are two good examples of the need, especially from the aspect of cost of management (or 'expense ratio' as it is called), for a constant review of the degree of effective decentralization which can be introduced, always remembering that the central management must still formulate policy and exert control by agreeing standards of performance with local managers against which achievement can be checked. A danger to be avoided is that a local manager or prospect manager or area manager – there is a host of titles for 'decentralized' managers – becomes so involved in administration which used to be done for him centrally that he loses touch with the urgencies of his job. If it is business-getting, for example, it can happen that a manager on whose shoulders the Head Office has placed a lot of additional control work will cease to be known both by his customers and his salesmen. Or if he is an outstanding engineer or technician he may well find himself caught up in a maze of administrative routine which prevents him from using his proper talent.

With every type of business operation, when its growth leads to decentralization, there is an increasing need for specialist services. The branch manager cannot be expected to control the Bank's reputation with the public at large by running his own public relations; the insurance branch manager cannot select and train his senior personnel; the manager of a local branch factory has not got time to undertake basic research. These specialist services must be arranged in such a way that they do not usurp a local manager's functions but, rather, enrich them.

There is a good deal of controversy nowadays among management experts on the question of 'specialist' responsibilities and the way such specialists should be integrated into the management operation. The Services concept of 'staff and line' involves considerable difficulties for business organization; the service managers, often exercising power without responsibility, tend to plug their own theories and gimmicks in isolation from the straightforward management task. Indeed the question of specialization, which begins so early nowadays in business training, means that more and more specialists are crowding in where there should be better and better managers. Earlier in this book the phrase 'opting for wider horizons' was used. Possibly the solution to the question is to ensure that all specialists have a proper grounding in management before deciding to concentrate on, say, industrial relations, or staffing, or organization and methods. While it would be wrong to suggest, in modern conditions, that there is no room for specialist services which spread across an entire organization, the man or woman whose views are most likely to be acceptable is the one who, having had some management experience, sees the specialist's role as being a tool, not a master of management.

A brief case history here will demonstrate some of the difficulties of specialist services. A large, highly diversified group was controlled from a central headquarters which contained in its staff a market research department set up to serve the constituent companies. Before this central service was established, however, a company within the group, largely concerned with exploring and satisfying consumer needs, had taken the initiative in engaging its own market research officer who, with a small staff, was slowly if somewhat painfully building up recognition among the different product managers of the value of his services. His salary and status in the operating company within the group was such that he could work on level terms and in close cooperation with those product managers. As a result he was able, over a period of years, not only to demonstrate the valuable contribution which could be made by the use of market survey techniques, but also to advise on day-to-day marketing problems. Acceptance of this advice on marketing matters came largely from the close relationship with the product managers which was carefully built up over the years. There was no possibility that a central research department at headquarters could ever achieve the same close liaison, partly because of a difference in location and partly, which is more important, because the immediate responsibility and loyalty of the central research staff was to their own top management rather than to that of the constituent company. Basically, the issue was one of confidence on the part of the product managers in the discretion of those from whom they sought advice.

Possibly one of the most urgent and overdue requirements for the larger business undertaking today is the establishment of an executive or a department to deal with matters of long-range planning. The British have been painfully slow to realize the importance of looking ahead. Ideally the man selected to do this vital job, to use his creative faculties to produce for the Board plans which, however frequently revised, will take heed of future changes, should be a potential chief executive. For it is he whose responsibility it must be to keep all branches of the business, line management and specialist services alike, alert to the need for self-criticism, for ceaseless inquiry into market standing, for vigilance in the matter of changing direction when it is proved that such change can alone keep a business dynamic and alive.

*

There are many arguments about decentralization in these days of mounting costs, and it is too big a subject to discuss in great detail. Since, however, it is the human aspect of management which permeates so much of the thinking in this book, it must be said that the problem of size, and hence the problem of responsible participation (a phrase used in an earlier chapter) by each and every worker, is a growing one. Management cannot shirk facing it. The 'organization man', more concerned with status than achievement, is an ugly manifestation of twentieth-century business. Much work in the U.S.A. and the U.K. is being done by great companies like Unilever, Tube Investments, General Motors, and I.C.I. to decentralize, and decentralize in such a way as to reduce the size of units to the point where employees can truly be said to be working *with* rather than working *for* management; and a good deal of new thinking, conditioned not least by high taxation, is being devoted to the wider question as to whether size is an inevitable consequence of business development. Though working for a really large organization carries with it certain consolations, of which the sense of security is the most potent, there are many today in the lower reaches of management who feel what amounts almost to a sense of claustrophobic and crushing anonymity as they pour out of huge factories or offices at the end of a day's work. How far decentralization can go towards resolving this human question is hard to say. Furthermore, the economics of running large production units must be considered – particularly in process industries where the unit is indivisible and plant has cost many millions of pounds. In such instances decentralization is virtually impossible.

The human problem can to some extent be solved by a system of effective communications, down and up, and sideways. This will at least assure that local managements do not feel out on a limb and that they can communicate that sense of belonging to those they are managing. Visits from directors and senior management; a constant flow of information about a company's work, aims, policies, and progress; 'house' magazines and staff newspapers; all these and other devices are essential if a highly decentralized organization is to be kept informed from manager to night watchman.

A Head Office tends to be regarded as some remote,

impersonal fastness peopled by soulless monsters. Many will remember the mistrustful attitude of the 'lower formation' to the 'higher formation' in the War, though this usually faded with promotion. 'Why, they're just like us!' used to be the surprised cry of the newcomer as he joined his former seniors. Management must be ready to accept this odd quirk of human nature. Strong as the temptation must often be for a harassed manager 'in the field' to inveigh against the Head Office staff, nothing can be more threatening to the achievement of a harmonious unit in a larger whole than a management that is forever criticizing the central organization.

The ability to communicate (and to make sure that those communicated to are conditioned to receive the communication) was discussed at the start of this book and assessed as an important management quality, but it needs to be more than a quality – it must be a management aim, consciously planned and carried out. Minimum interference but maximum communication might well be said to summarize what a central management, managing its decentralized units, should work for.

There is a point here for the student of human relations to ponder. It is odd that, while imaginative managements go to considerable pains to get among employees, to listen to their problems, and to discuss suggestions, it is rare for an employee to ask a manager anything about *his* problems. Communication is, by definition, a two-way affair, but it seldom works that way. Is it perhaps a fact that employees are plainly uninterested and, though receptive to anything management cares to produce for them in the way of literature about the Company, find it hard to make the running themselves? Experience of Joint Councils, at which management and work-people meet together under minimum restraint, shows that the stimulus for discussion and action must more often than not come from those in authority. Shop floor representatives seem reluctant to take the Board seats that are being offered to them in increasing numbers. The stimulus for constructive discussion has to come more often than not from the top.

*

At any point in a management situation the need to co-ordinate functions is essential. An organization chart can point the way and a complex network of committees can be organized. But charts and committees are worthless if management posts are not filled by men and women who are seized with the fact that responsibility, to be effective, must be shared.

It is the man or woman at the head of an operation who must set the pace in the matter of coordination. He or she needs to appreciate that people working in a vacuum quickly get out of touch. 'Keeping people in the picture', for all the slightly comic associations of the phrase, is more than a question of communication: it is also the ability to arrange matters in such a way that overlapping of function is avoided and, equally important, that no management task is carried out in isolation. An earlier chapter has stressed that industrial management has to be concerned with three factors which are, broadly, production, marketing, and finance. This is a trinity of interests. That each should have its due and that there should be the strictest attention to ensuring that these basic functions are coordinated is the chief executive's priority. He will achieve his end in different ways and it is wrong to dogmatize. In some businesses, management by committee has been successful: in others some other co-ordinating machinery, less cumbersome and time-consuming than the committee method, works better. This may consist of clear statements of policy and action by the Chief Executive and the top management team, distributed widely. The aim, however it is secured, must be to avoid purposeless effort because A is unaware of what B is doing.

Coordination of effort, above all, needs to be thought through. A move to a new factory or office, or the launching of a product, two straightforward management problems taken as examples, can only be speedy and effective if, in advance of the operation, everybody's part in it is phased in, clearly stated, and understood in advance.

*

'The Business of Management' was an ambitious title for a chapter. It presupposed a kind of know-how that can be captured in words and set down. In point of fact, managerial inspiration – the driving force that *really* makes people do things and achieve objectives – is transmitted by the determination and character of the manager. It is no good closing one's eyes to the fact. But management can undoubtedly derive much from a calm appreciation of possibly not more than four basic points which, if constantly borne in mind, can help towards the creation of the sort of conditions in which effective management can function. These are: first, the objectives must be clearly stated; secondly, responsibilities must be defined and accepted; thirdly, communication must be two-way or even three-way; fourthly, the chief executives in any enterprise, of whatever size, must always control and progress the operation, accepting that there are many well-tested techniques (of which intelligent use of information from a computer is one) to enable controls to be sensibly planned. The words used in this chapter – organization, delegation, control, decentralization, communications, coordination – are potent factors in the business of management. But they are dead, meaningless words unless a sense of high purpose is breathed into them. A business is the reflection of the people within it. It cannot be said too often that the most sophisticated computer that technology can produce fails utterly to vindicate its use if ordinary mortals charged with programming the information required fail to comprehend their task.

5

Management for Whom?

IN the last thirty years, during which the Second World War was the great catalyst, the role of management, especially in Western Europe, has changed profoundly. In thinking about management ends it is essential to examine how this change has come about. Management, instead of being the task of men and women who made their decisions in an atmosphere pretty well insulated from the political, economic, and social conditions around them, has had to change course entirely. It is not overstating the case to describe the present-day conception of management as a social science. Technical, commercial and even financial factors are no longer the only – and no longer indeed the really compelling – ones which management has to understand before taking action. It is the human motivations – the motivations of the managed and the markets – even of the political masters – that management must grasp if it is to succeed in the new conditions. Why is this and how has all this come about?

To appreciate what has happened since the late thirties it is necessary to look at the question from three angles – political, economic, and social – and relate the vast developments in each field to the management question.

Stating briefly the chief political developments: the Second World War brought about the emergence of two great blocs, the East and the West, and, concurrently, the political weakening of the former European imperialist powers. This shift in the balance of world power has had the effect of making a weakened Europe far more interested in economic development than in its former preoccupation with political and administrative matters both within itself and *vis-à-vis* Asia and Africa. Although the rivalry between Russia and the U.S.A., with Chinese aspirations looming like a huge interrogation mark over both, for the allegiance of the world dominates the political scene, the awakening political consciousness of the masses everywhere has had a progressive effect in the renewal of systems of government.

Traditional systems have given place to new forms which, often, have a basis in emotion and unquestioned authority: dictators, near-dictators, and military groups have been having their day. While the European nations have been contracting their political power so have the hitherto European-dominated 'colonies' begun to emerge politically and industrially. Nationalism has become a creed of incalculable importance. It is, perhaps, an inconsistency that, combined with this political incoherence, which is a world phenomenon, economic development has steadily advanced. Reasons are not too hard to see. The war accelerated technological development which in turn meant a rise in productivity and an increase in available energy. Labour has been divided to a greater degree and, on the distribution front, channels have been lengthened to look after the widening distances between markets and centres of production. This has produced a higher standard of living for the masses and, as a result, a readjustment of the social scale: though there is still a long way to go, the gap between the 'haves' and the 'have-nots' is narrowing.

But as this economic development has taken place so has there been a rise in the degree of government involvement in the normal course of business events. Governments are no longer able to stand aside and simply govern. Two factors, above all others, have underpinned government authority: defence, now a diminishing factor, and, especially in Britain, the growth of the doctrine of full and stable employment with which, a shade paradoxically, is coupled successive

British Governments' yearning to keep the wages-prices spiral in some sort of control and create a favourable balance of payments.

The economic consequences of these factors must be briefly summarized; a realistic (if that is the word) defence programme has meant State influence in questions both of the production and the spread of wealth; so far as social aims are concerned – and especially full and stable employment – governments are becoming more and more committed to legislation which fixes the framework of economic activity. Taxation, international negotiations and agreements, controls of exchange rates, attention to areas of under-employment, control of mergers and monopolies – all those purely governmental responsibilities when related to the giddy pace of technological progress and the resultant growth of wealth have led to social changes of immense importance. In the main, populations everywhere are growing, are better fed, and live more comfortably: this is not to say that there are not still great areas of sub-standard, near-subsistence living, but even in Africa and South-East Asia, the drift towards the towns is surely an expression of mankind's discovery of the, sometimes dubious, joys of communal living, shared security, and material prosperity. It follows that more sophisticated communities, anxious to consolidate this newly-won improvement in standards of living, are susceptible to all kinds of organizations which will protect their situations. Trade unions, trade associations, economically-tied groups – these are direct results of the social changes which on the one hand bring with them an overdue recognition of the principles of social justice but, on the other, place an even greater responsibility on the shoulders of leaders, in all fields of activity, to ensure that a preoccupation with security and prosperity will not result in even greater insecurity and ultimate extinction.

Not very long ago a leading industrialist, examining the

rate of the development of management within the broad context of human problems of industry, analysed the reasons for the acceleration in pace as:

First the intense pressure for greater production arising initially from post-war demands and the need to re-establish national balanced economies: these were followed by demands that are growing all over the world for better material standards of living.

Secondly, the acceleration of technological development which is often called a second Industrial Revolution, and the increase in size and complexity of industrial organizations which accompanies it.

Thirdly, technological development and increasing production have created the need for newer patterns and techniques of management.

Fourthly, the social conscience of industry has developed considerably and there has been increasing public interest in management particularly in areas of frequent industrial unrest.

Finally, full employment with its manifest advantages for public well-being and the development of social democracy have brought about a set of circumstances which have never been experienced by management.

These are admirably expressed and form a suitable link between the wider examination of the past thirty years with which this chapter began and the detailed considerations it must try to solve.

*

In the context of 'Management for Whom', it is necessary to examine the effect of these developments – economic and social – on mangement itself and to try to draw some conclusions. In today's conditions of trade, finance, and industry there are many participants, shareholders, employees, the consumer, the community, and the State. It is virtually impossible to isolate any one of these. Management, if it accepts its twentieth-century functions, is caught up in a mesh of widening responsibility.

In a previous chapter a management function was referred to as making the best possible use of man, material, and methods. To this function must be added the responsibility for thinking ahead in a world that is on the move and in which the contentment – even fulfilment – of the individual employee is accepted as a prime management task. Management, if its functions as set out in this paragraph are accepted, has surely got to combine the efficient handling of men and materials with a suitable organization that will result in maximum internal harmony and which will supply at a reasonable profit goods and service to the satisfaction of an always expanding number of users. However this management function is looked at, whatever the emphasis, not only are managers human but so are those for whom they are managing, and it is surely important then to consider first the impact of management on people.

In seeking to find some answers in relation to people rather than things, let the shareholders be first considered. With the spread of income there has been an upsurge of investment, public, institutional, and private, and the word investment must be taken to include savings. Management can no longer ignore these legions who, be they employees or virtually anonymous outside bodies and individuals, have a stake in a business undertaking. Ignoring the most obvious example – a government's responsibility to *its* shareholders, the taxpayers – business ownership has been widened enormously in the last twenty years as a direct consequence of those issues discussed earlier in this chapter – the growth and distribution of wealth arising from full and stable employment as well as the rate of technical development which, in its turn, means a considerable increase in numbers of higher-paid skilled workers. In the U.K. alone it is estimated that, directly and indirectly, three out of four adults are investors. They are indirect investors by virtue, for example, of being members of pension schemes, trade unions, building societies, unit trusts, banks, and insurance companies. The direct investors in the United Kingdom are those who themselves hold shares in companies or the government; these are now believed to number about $4\frac{1}{2}$-5,000,000 – a number that is steadily growing.

It is not fortuitous that the less austere as well as the more respectable Sunday newspapers in Great Britain now write informative pieces about the stock markets or that the B.B.C. devotes time to news of the Stock Exchange. *The Times* which, until Lord Thomson's purchase of it, had somewhat muffled its business news, now for example publishes a daily Business Supplement which, if not consistently accurate, at least supplies the seemingly insatiable appetite of a growing public with a flow of business detail ranging from the private lives of tycoons to more mundane comment on trading results. The fact of the growth of shareholding (and the great success of the unit trust movement must be noted in this connexion) means that management can no longer pursue its private path. A take-over bid, the resignation of a chairman, the securing (or the loss) of a big international contract, the 'face of the firm' – its advertising, its design policy, its delivery vans, etc. – are all questions of increasing public interest not simply because they are news-worthy but because the small investor, no less than the larger one, is becoming directly and personally interested.

Management for shareholders in the private sectors rests on the existence of a liberal, capitalistic society; shareholders' money is essential to the development plans of forward-looking enterprises. It is only in the muddier fields of nationalized industries – in Britain, coal, electricity, gas, the railways, steel and so on – that the matter of managing in the shareholders' interests becomes a question of government policy.

Management today may well be criticized for taking too little notice of shareholders. The shareholders are the sinews of business and, as such, deserve the closest attention. In the scramble to secure staff and labour under conditions of virtually full employment too many companies tend to think exclusively of, for example, employee welfare, while forgetting the equally pressing question of the welfare of the shareholders. This is especially true of the private sector but no less relevant where public ownership is concerned. Shareholders should be regarded as partners in business enterprise but how often does this happen and to what extent is it the fault of shareholders themselves? Management, and especially boards of directors, tend to be over-secretive about their trading results and treat shareholders as if they were a necessary evil. This is particularly true in Great Britain: in the U.S.A. the situation is better and managements are far less inhibited in their quarterly, six-monthly, and annual statements covering every aspect of the business. In Britain the average Annual General Meeting gives an impression of a direction anxious to get it over and done with as fast as possible and questions from shareholders are treated as if they were somehow in poor taste. There are, of course, shining exceptions to this discouraging side of the story. Better produced, more frequent, informative, and readable Chairman's Speeches and Company Accounts are being produced in a growing number of instances, and shareholders themselves are beginning to realize their own interest in identification and organizations in which they own a part. They, too, have in the past been far too remote from the problem. There are even examples – far too rare today – of managements encouraging shareholders to promote the goods or services manufactured by the companies in which they are investors as well as to visit the factories or offices where such goods and services are prepared.

Recent Finance Acts have called upon managements of public companies to reveal a great deal more than hitherto in their Annual Balance Sheets. This has been a good development though the press, alas, seem to have derived most pleasure, once such informative Balance Sheets are published, from publicising league tables of top management salaries and forgetting (or perhaps overlooking) far more significant data from the shareholder's standpoint. It may be that Sir XYZ is the highest paid Chairman in the country but what is the price/earnings ratio of his company?

Before the war many companies were run autocratically by an individual or by a small executive board with complete disregard for the interests of the shareholders as distinct from those of the company itself. The true profits were not disclosed and dividend policy was frequently not related to profits but rather to keeping the shareholders quiet. Many such businesses were successful but in a few cases the situation was abused and shareholders lost their money. The situation is now completely changed. The law, as we have said, has been altered to require more disclosure of trading facts. Further the big increase in the shareholding public has forced recognition of the fact that democratic principles involve a full acceptance by the management of the right of shareholders to be treated as partners in the business. Before the war there was considerable justification for withholding a large part of the profits from the shareholders and for reinvesting this money in the business. Any company must retain sufficient cash to maintain its place against competing business and this will usually involve a substantial retention of profits to supplement the cash provided by depreciation provisions. If, however, the management of a good company has big plans for expansion it will not be afraid to ask shareholders to put up more capital. It can be of immense help to any company to disclose freely how the business is faring, to pay generous dividends, and to ask the shareholders for more capital whenever there are developments which cannot be financed by a moderate retention of profits. The shareholders own the company and managements must recognize this fact, and while it is true that the shareholders can always sell out and are thus not nearly as committed as employees or customers it is no excuse for the neglect of their interests or for their own apathy – both being present-day characteristics.

*

It might well be claimed that the importance of management for the worker is self-evident and hardly needs elaboration. The theme of this book is, after all, leadership in management, and the securing of responsible participation throughout a business operation is management's highest aim. For precisely those reasons, social, economic, and political, which were briefly discussed earlier in this chapter and which characterize the post-Second-World-War period the employee is no longer a name in the salary ledger or on the pay packet: he or she is a sentient human being passionately concerned with getting a square deal.

It must be categorically stated that, however managers might like to evade the issue, the question of money reward for a job done remains a worker's absolute priority. This may be a glimpse of the obvious but it is often forgotten. Man is a social animal: his personal comfort and security and the welfare of those for whom he is immediately responsible are his first consideration. However varied and imaginative the additional benefits may be that are dreamed up by management, however basic the job satisfaction, however enlightened the leadership he is offered, the actual cash received for services rendered remains for the great majority the most important factor. Trade Unions have achieved formidable results in those fields of work which are amenable to trade union organization and the relations of management to the unions will be discussed later. There still remain, the world over, millions of work-people (in the widest sense of the word) who depend wholly on management's appreciation of the need to examine, ceaselessly and realistically, the wage requirement of those who are not so organized.

Managements are guilty in that too little job evaluation is carried out in all fields of industry and commerce. If it is true that management is a continuous process, good management means the acceptance of responsibility all the way down the line. The question of this constant measurement of a job's part in the business scheme and relating it to an adequate reward, is a task which must be delegated by those who have made sure that those responsible are themselves properly paid. Management for the worker is then a question of social obligation. It is not enough to evolve pay scales and hope to get away with them. The initiative must always remain with the managers – if the managers are imbued with a sense of obligation it is not unlikely that they themselves will get their just rewards.

It may well be asked what *is* fair pay? There are no easy formulae. A number of factors enter into the calculation. The kind of work, the degree of responsibility, working conditions, security of employment, degrees of skill – all these and a host more – contribute to the evolution of proper pay scales. And the State itself with its cost-of-living indices, its taxation, and its aim of full employment cannot stand aside from this question – the State which has itself become an employer on so vast a scale. It is perhaps an over-simplification at which economists would possibly shudder to say that, given the primary fact of the need for a minimum wage which will secure at least two of the four freedoms – from want and from fear – the facts of trade and the labour market itself will look after the rest of the problem. But even when that is admitted there are variations within the limits of what the market can afford which call upon management's best endeavours to ensure that there are proper rewards for those who merit them.

This emphasis upon pay should not overshadow management's other obligations towards those who are being managed. It is simply placed first because in fact it is the first consideration. A swollen pay packet – acceptable as it may be – earned in conditions of squalor, of gross discomfort, of shop floor tyranny, or of doubtful security will always recoil on a management. Hence the preoccupation with conditions of working and with what is loosely called 'welfare'. Even if it is argued that the finest Works Canteen or Sick Bay is no substitute for money – money, that is to say, that is under one's own control to spend as one pleases – there is a growing acceptance by management of the need to make conditions of work less discouraging than they used to be. There are fine shades to this question of staff welfare. Take the Cadbury organization at Bournville (or Lever Brothers at Port Sunlight) with their model village and staff amenities generally. Here is consideration for the employee carried to immense and stimulating lengths. But one is forced to wonder whether, in fact, the encroachment of management into the private lives of employees is, in the long run, desirable. Cadbury's record of staff turnover at their gigantic Bournville plants is impressively low. Perhaps the answer is that there will always be those who are prepared to surrender up something for the advantages of a conforming, community existence even when that community is exclusively concerned with the same kind of job under the same employer subject to quite a lot of local rules.

That management should be concerned with the elimination of ugliness within its offices and factories is beyond argument. Here there are immense fields to conquer in a battle which starts from the design of factory and office buildings to the minutiae of good pictures on office walls, amenities that are sightly, decent colour schemes, and all the rest of it. This is a form of welfare that is not only enlightened but that pays dividends.

The matter of retirement is also often taken too casually by management. A sudden transition from a full working day to no work at all can break a worker's spirit. A gradual phasing-out of responsibilities so that the blow falls less hard is one answer to a question which becomes more urgent as technological advancement threatens the status and responsibilities of older men. The government has played an increasing part in this matter. Redundancy payments and retraining schemes are two developments indicating that thought is being given to a highly complicated problem.

With the growing self-consciousness about management ends and means that has been accelerated by events since the Second World War, many wise and dedicated people have been studying the relationship of pay to other incentives. The abrupt statement at the start of this section that pay is the first priority needs qualification – qualification in the sense that work is compounded of many factors of which personal satisfaction and recognition of achievement are two constituents. A later chapter will be tackling the question of whether management can make people work better and it will be more appropriate to discuss incentives in that context. But it can be said at this point, even if it is repeated later, that management must face up to the unattractive fact that the majority of workers feel little sense of involvement in the company in which they are working. Their interest is primarily self-interest because their basic loyalties as free people in a free society must be to outside, more personal interests, be they family, hobbies, religion, or friends. Management's job here is clear. It must be to manage so effectively and to ensure that the work flow is so planned that the worker's first priority, adequate pay for work done, is properly met. Management leadership must accept all the responsibility for seeing this is done. It is only when this is achieved that something akin to loyalty can be expected of the worker – loyalty and, more important still, a sense of what Drucker calls 'willing dedication'.

By way of postscript: it would be interesting to be allowed a Wellsian peep at the next fifty years in the matter of management for the employee. While today the question of equitable payment for work done, provided always there is a degree of job satisfaction, is an employee's priority, new factors may be gradually changing the situation. Overall improved standards of living, growth of leisure, a completer view of the good things beyond the immediacies – these may all eventually contribute to a new assessment of ambition, of the motive of work. It is tempting to be starry-eyed about new incentives and new values. Management can anticipate these values by recognizing that the fuller life is now no longer the possession of a few and a re-examination of 'What's it all for' must start within management itself.

*

In Great Britain especially, the somewhat belated realization that the finest management in the world is wasted if its products and services are not distributed and consumed has come about largely for the reasons set out at the start of this chapter. The rise in the standard of living – the tempo of living itself – which the last twenty-five years have brought about, has meant that customers for all sorts of goods and every kind of service, from an atomic reactor via banking and insurance to a razor blade, are questing and critical. A fuller examination into the complex of marketing belongs more appropriately to another chapter but if one is thinking of management ends in relation to people, this question of consumers must be discussed here.*

So far as management in Great Britain particularly is concerned the customer has fortunately now become a vital factor. The sanctions upon which either nineteenth-century Free Trade or early-twentieth-century protectionist trade rested no longer exist. These islands have lost the advantages of superiority at sea, in industrialization, and in Europe's strong dependence on our exports. The maintenance of our export trade and the existence of a robust home market are indivisible. Customers everywhere – with export customers as priorities – are essential to Britain's survival and her declared objectives of social justice and well-being. Management must, therefore, face the fact that the former attitude of 'this is what we produce: take it or leave it' must be replaced by urgent concern with what the consumer really needs. It is not adventitious that in those countries where the consumer's needs have had prodigious attention paid to them there have been equally prodigious management successes. And, it must be fairly recorded, there are outstanding exceptions in Great Britain to this, generally, gloomy story; British taste and public requirements are changing very rapidly as a result of the levelling up of society. Easier credit, for example, has had a fascinating effect on how people spend their money. In Britain one has only to talk to a publican to be reminded of the fact that what used to be spent on somewhat ephemeral items is now allocated to the payment of instalments on television sets and washing machines. This is

---

*Peter Drucker in his exuberant *The Practice of Management* (Heinemann) says 'If we want to know what a business is we have to start with its *purpose*. And its purpose must be outside of the business itself. In fact it must lie in society, since a business enterprise is an organ of society. There is only one valid definition of business purpose: to *create a customer*.' This is discussed in detail in Chapter One.

not to present a picture of a tobacco- and alcohol-starved Britain. Far from it. But it is proved that the shift from purely 'consumable goods' to 'consumer durables' is a significant factor in the public's spending. As a barmaid rather wistfully put it 'there are no really serious drinkers in my pub nowadays'.

There are, however, dilemmas for management here. Too much attention to customer requirements could result in a lowering of standards in design, performance, and service. Truly enlightened management must have the courage of its own convictions. It must be a jump ahead of public taste and requirement. It must lead rather than follow. How can management square the need – the compulsive, commercial need – to give the consumers what they want today with what research and imaginative development indicate should be wanted tomorrow? Or, put another way, is it a matter of the lowest common multiple or the highest common factor?

The lesson for management is surely clear. It must continue to extend the field of its attention beyond the shareholders and employees to the users of its products and services. The foreman no less than the managing director must convey his enthusiasm and belief in what he is offering outside his immediate circle. It is true of course that all the conventional and unconventional methods of sales promotion, salesmanship at all levels, public and trade advertising, sales literature, and the rest – can go a long way towards the creation of an image. These are being used with increasing vigour but in the end it is a compound of planned marketing, of fitness for purpose, and the belief that employees and especially the sales personnel have in a service or product that wins the consumer to its use. Management, in concerning itself with consumers, has a great responsibility in those matters. Advertising claims must be honest, promotion must be balanced and the sales effort sustained.

It is interesting that there has been a marked increase, since the war, in the initiative taken by the consumers themselves to make sure that managements who are serving them are, so to speak, serving them properly. Normally a manufacturer has a large organization behind him whereas the consumer has precious little backing other than his or her own judgement. Weights and Measures, Safety, Standards, informative labelling, reliable performance, advertising claims – this is a small sample of subjects upon which, surprisingly, the consumer aided by a highly articulate Press, Consumer Protection movements, and a host of other devices now demands help and advice. It is arguable that powerful groups like the Consumers' Union in the United States, Statens Konsumentrad in Sweden, or the Consumer bodies in Great Britain should never have been necessary and that managements should be for ever on the alert to see that they, rather than consumers, are in charge of the situation. On the other hand there must be many instances where a properly organized consumers' council can give invaluable advice to management whose attitude should be to encourage such help. Managers, living daily with their problems, tend to be too close to them. A mixture of cooperation from and service to the consumer should be a management ideal. Management is as much dependent on consumers as on shareholders and employees. It is a trinity of interests.

Management must keep in proportion the assertion that because freedom of choice is desirable in a relatively free economy it is therefore up to the consumer to exercise his or her own judgement. The argument continues along the lines of assuming that any sort of consumer protection is an unwarranted intrusion into the citadels of free enterprise. As a postscript to all this, it is often the sanguine conclusion that because bad merchandise or ineffective services are bad business, the consumer need never fear exploitation. This is specious and it doesn't work. Shoddy goods and services that are incomplete or ill-conceived are the direct consequences of this material age when so many consumers, suddenly aware of what money can buy, are fobbed off with the second best because they, the consumers, know no better. It would be nice to think that the second best is doomed to a short life. It is unfortunately not so. There are still too many goods and services that are but marginally effective. Although it has its critics the Consumer Council, set up in 1963, is doing a worth-while job. It acts as a watchdog and it is unquestionable that the evidence it collects in the consumer's interest is taken seriously by manufacturers and purveyors of services alike. The Consumer's Association, with its magazine *Which?* also plays a useful role. *Which?* might be assailed for being primarily of service to the middle-class consumer, but its overall readership assessed today at 5,250,000 suggests that its following is a wide one. The fact that public libraries subscribe to it probably mitigates the accusation that it only meets middle-class interests.

*

More and more shareholders, employees, and consumers become involved in industry and commerce, and management finds itself unable to remain insulated from the interests of the community at large. The fact that so many able and thoughtful people from the Commonwealth and Empire under the leadership of H.R.H. the Duke of Edinburgh have spent time, and will be spending some more, on the human problems of industrial communities gives point to this particular subject. In North America it is also a question which is constantly under review. It is a truism that the growth of industry and commerce has brought with it both blessings and curses to the community; in parenthesis, it is to be hoped that countries on the verge of development will absorb with the minimum pain the lessons learnt the hard way by the countries that are today great industrial communities.

As it is the community that supplies the working force for management to manage and, indeed, that supplies managers themselves, it is important to make a distinction between management for employees, discussed in a previous section, and management for the community as a whole. The community, is today, vitally concerned with industry and commerce, the appearance and reputation of a local factory, the service in neighbourhood shops, the morale of those members of the community who are in local employ – these are questions in which the community is interested. Management cannot ignore this interest. From a recruiting aspect alone it must aim to make itself an accepted part of the scene: it must be jealous of its reputation: it must be identified with the character and aspirations of the district in which it is located.

Managers have also a very special duty to the community to ensure that business planning is constantly aware of the danger of economic breakdown which can inflict irreparable wounds. Britain is getting very used to the idea of virtually full employment and it is well that this should be so, but it is more than a governmental responsibility to make sure that the thirties never happen again. The community itself has a vested interest in full employment. Drastic reorganization – especially in areas where there is a single industry – or an ostrich-like disregard of dwindling or changing markets can quickly bring about personal tragedy and upheaval. It is true that diversification of industry and the broadening of the base of the economy have done much to help the communities in the depressed areas as well as to eliminate the worst risks, but the threat is always just around the corner. Managements can never afford to be complacent and money must be spent in looking ahead.

Though a later discussion of 'Management of What' will have to consider the question of machines, automation, shift working, and the like, in the present context a moment must be spent on the problem of shift work as it affects the community. Industry and commerce, in these post-war years of immense development, make different demands on people's time. The routine worker can plan his or her leisure, but the shift worker with odd working hours makes claims on parents, housewives, and landladies which place managements greatly in their debt. Is this debt acknowledged? Does management trouble itself sufficiently, for example, about the effects of the comings and goings at all hours on the family life, routine, unity, and social life?

And morale? It is one thing to write about the need to preserve the morale of the employee himself, but how much does management think about the disastrous effect on those outside the factory or office gates – family, friends, and sweethearts – of the disgruntled men or women whose regard for management is bitter and resentful? Management's responsibility here is clear. Managers must realize that the range of their management must look after the *total* human situation of which morale – twenty-four hours a day morale that is – is a prime part.

Much of the foregoing has been generalization – relevant generalization perhaps but generalization. It would be worth taking a specific case of where management has to think about its relationship with the community: a small example it is true but an interesting one which was highlighted some years ago by Lord Pilkington, a former President of what is now the Confederation of British Industries. Take the question of playing fields and recreation in many industrial towns. Local companies with greater resources find themselves in many cases able to provide better amenities for their workpeople than the community. Often there has been a long history of financial difficulties and the independent clubs, be they of church or other foundation, relying on enthusiasts, just have not had the money to produce the amenities which the big local firm or firms supply in generous and subsidized quantities exclusively for their staffs and families. Let Lord Pilkington's questions be asked as he asked them for they pinpoint problems for management which are entirely to the point. Is this a good thing for the community or not? Does it help to develop an association outside work between those who are employed in the large firms and the rest, or does it tend to increase the *mutually exclusive* relationship? Is the standard of recreational facilities a deciding factor when young men are deciding on a career, or must the firm do it in a competitive spirit regardless of the effect on the community? Or is it so important that a decent firm must go far beyond the standard the ordinary clubs in the town could afford? Management, relating itself to those around it, has got to answer that kind of problem.

Maybe there is no one answer. Solutions alter with differing circumstances. The town of Corby which until 1934 was a village has today, thanks to the establishment of an iron and steel works in that year, a population nearing 50,000. Houses, sports fields, and other amenities had to be provided by the company, but as the community develops, encouraged by the company, local initiative should be developing local amenities. How, for example, to adjust the problems of differing rents between Company-subsidized houses and those provided by the Town Council? That is one aspect. These are cases, especially overseas, where a community development is completely separated from the dominating local employer and where it is believed that the best 'sense of community' can be assured in this way.

A group recently studying the playing field problem came quite simply to the conclusion that the proper answer to the question was simply that the management of an individual company, using its judgement and at the psychological moment, should hand over its fields for the use of the community.

There is a further aspect of managing for the community

which deserves consideration. That is the matter of company executives identifying themselves with public and local interests by doing voluntary service. Local Government, for example, needs more and more the help of trained minds and, in Britain especially, there are a great number of institutions and organizations completely dependent on unpaid assistance. Is it not management's task to make sure that such time will in fact be available? 'Don't bother me', 'I mind my own business' is so often the plaint of the overworked manager, who at the end of the day, shuts himself off from every sort of social obligation. This is wrong. The duty of management to the community in this aspect is clear: business organization should be such that time is made for such service to be possible.

Mutually exclusive: those two words really contain within them the nub of the matter of management for the community. The truth surely is that industry and commerce (and, hence, industrial and commercial management) and the community cannot any longer be mutually exclusive. Both sides must get on with their allotted tasks – industry and commerce to prosper in the interests of the community and the community to develop its character and social life in the interest of the businesses that flourish within it. In industrial and commercial society today nobody can really pursue a set of entirely exclusive interests: the pace and ramifications of modern life make this so.

*

In writing of business management and the State there is a risk that the emphasis might be placed the wrong way round: that is to say on how the State manages for business. The workings of the State are so apparent everywhere and the tentacles of government reach into so many business activities that management, even should it wish to go its own way, cannot ignore this most important of all post-Second

World War trends. The 'public sector' as it is rather grimly called, and the way it is financed, staffed, and developed, is a force which the rest of industry and commerce can no longer disregard. It is, in fact, often complementary to it. Large State undertakings become customers of smaller, private ones; conversely, the 'private sector' depends increasingly on the services which the 'public sector' supplies. Fuel, power, and transport are examples.

The growth of the great State Corporations in Britain like the Port of London Authority, the B.B.C., or the London Transport Executive and the development of the nationalized undertakings such as the National Coal Board, the Central Electricity Authority, British Rail, and the Bank of England are examples of how the State, in addition to its responsiblities for the great political issues of Defence, Education, and a host of others, is also committed on behalf of State enterprises to the creation of an economic framework within which management has got to work. When the framework is well contrived it can be of great assistance to management, but when it is bungled it can disastrously affect management's task. Consider the control of inflation. However hard managements may try they are powerless, in the grip of State mismanagement, mistiming, or miscalculation, to check what the economists can diagnose but are not quite sure how to cure. Or a strike in a nationalized undertaking with its paralysing effect on normal trading routine. Or the relative effects of different instruments of Government policy – monetary, fiscal, controls – which can either encourage or discourage a business development.

But this section is not concerned with the way the State behaves or misbehaves in the matter of the economy. Politicians have written, spoken, and debated billions of words in defence of their policies and the final sanction in the West rests with the voter. The task here is, rather, to analyse what business managements should do about the State – not what the State should do about them.

One must be careful of words. The State and the Community are really one. With the increase of Government intervention in everyday affairs it has become customary to think of the Government as the State with disquieting undertones of the totalitarian countries in mind. That this confusion exists is not surprising; governments, not so much the politicians but the civil servants, tend, more and more, to become anonymous and faceless as their influence becomes the more pervasive.

The previous section looked at management's relations with the Community in a narrower almost a 'neighbourhood' context. The Esso Petroleum Company in a document *Where We Stand* combines the Community and the State very realistically and writes:

Since a company is an integral part of the social and economic life of the community – be it locally or nationally – it is under an obligation to conduct its business in such a way as to further the social and economic progress of the community, or at very least not to impede it.

It has a duty beyond its immediate business of supplying goods at the right quality and price; it has a duty of citizenship, of co-operating with the proper authorities at every level of government. In framing its policies, it must consider the wider aspects of the public interest. In its everyday actions it must practise consideration for its neighbours. It must be an active asset to the community within which it operates, not a passive occupier of space.

These are noble aims. How, in fact, does a business management 'further the social and economic progress of the community' other than by supplying it with something it wants at the right price?

The first answer must be that management has a responsibility to make profits so that it can create more wealth and pay more taxes. The operation of 'furthering the social and economic progress of the community' must be a profitable one. Industry and commerce are not accountable to the State to be so, i.e. profitable, but in a liberal, capitalistic, competitive society business will not exist long if it is not. It follows then that those concerned with good management, accepting, as they must do, the validity of the 'ends' of much of any democratically elected government's aims for the community (even if there are differences about means) are inextricably bound up with the State as such. The pity is that politicians (hence the State) mortgage the wealth before it is earned. Doing good for the community is an intoxicating business which can go to a government's head. How far does management organize itself to keep the elected representatives and their servants on the rails?

It is surely not an exaggeration that the quality of management and the efficiency with which it is carried out must, in its turn, greatly affect the attitude of the government of the day. The desire of governments to enter legitimate fields for private enterprise – and in Britain this problem is a recurrent one – is inflamed when managements fail. And management can get little but cold comfort from the depressing spectacle of State enterprises which do not, in the event, produce better labour relations, administrative efficiency, and improved services to the consumer. These are political matters with which top management at least should be concerned. Though the ranks particularly those of industrialists seconded to state concerns are growing, too few able business men are prepared to give time either to politics, to voluntary or part-time paid national work. It is the same small band of overworked patriots (for that is what they are) who are to be seen 'chairing' committees, sitting on public bodies, giving part-time meagrely paid service to State boards. The rewards? There is a passage in *The Boss: the Life and Times of the British Business Man*, by Roy Lewis and Rosemary Stewart, which well describes them:

... those who wish for public recognition have to seek it outside business – in politics, public works, or philanthropy. This search may have unfortunate effects for their subordinates: the business whose chairman or managing director is kept waiting for a public honour, which he feels has been too long delayed, is likely to suffer from a rapid turnover of top executives. Sir John, unless he now wishes to become Lord, is often a much more relaxed and easy man to work for. 'Gongs' have in the past not been awarded for business success as such; only for the good which a man has done with the money he has made, or the influence he has secured. This is tending to change, and many business men wish the change could be speeded up, arguing that to do the necessary outside committee work, like the vigil before knighthood in medieval times, is rather meaningless and distracts a man from his proper job. They say that now there is so little to be made out of business, it should, in the matter of honours, be put on more of an equality with the civil service. They argue that their productive record may be as good as, or better than, that of many civil servants, and probably worth far more to the nation than the running of a few philanthropic works. 'Just because Bill runs the Homes for Khaki British babies,' they growl, 'he gets his K. What about those two power stations I got for British industry in Byelo-Russia this year? A cool ten millions. Don't they think that's worth anything?'

There is now plenty of evidence that this attitude is beginning to change. The introduction of the Queen's Award to Industry and the recognition, in various ways, of, for example, men and women who have done outstanding work for export is encouraging. There are many people who view the somewhat mystical system of British honours and awards with wry scepticism, but such a system is a small price to pay for a worth-while return.

*

In the export field there is much scope for management to do its duty by the State. A truism which cannot be written down too often is that Britain's export trade and her survival are indivisible. It is a fact that half Britain's exports are accounted for by only 120 firms. This is indication enough of the urgent need for more and more business managements to examine export possibilities with an end which might be described as truly enlightened self-interest. This is no place to discuss the problems and possibilities of export.* It is merely to suggest that a great deal of new thinking by both management and the Government needs to be done if Britain is not to slip behind in the race for world trade.

*

This chapter 'Management for Whom?' opens up fields of thought which extend far beyond the inevitably limited number of points which have been made in previous sections. In the end this is an ideological matter in a world where ideologies are in perpetual conflict. A duty of management in the society the non-Communist world surely wishes to create for itself is to sit permanently in judgement on itself. Few would disagree with Erwin Canham when he said at a Harvard Conference, 'The only valid social goal is improvement of the lot of man and the better relationship of men to one another and to God, to fundamental truth.' Is management, in the way it manages for its shareholders, its consumers, its employees, and the Community/State, going in the direction of that goal? The technological progress of the last twenty years, to which is linked ever-increasing production, may be leading to too great a preoccupation with the satisfaction of material wants. Accepting that it is to serve the community in the widest possible sense that management must be dedicated, must it not be ever vigilant to avoid materialism's worst evils?

* See next chapter, 'The Export Challenge'.

6

Management of What?

PREVIOUS chapters have been concerned with people – the people who are directly and indirectly affected by managerial skill. Satisfying the shareholders, serving the consumers, contributing to the welfare of the community, accepting the responsibility for seeing that employees are rewardingly employed – these are management ends. And these human ends have to be linked with means which, though still dependent, as everything must be dependent, on the human element, are subjects which have to be considered separately. The three chief management means are Finance, Production, and Marketing. Common to all three is, of course, the management of personnel, but this is not being treated as a separate management function because the relations between manager and managed, the real stuff of management, are the background against which this book is set.

FINANCE

This is an accountant-dominated age. That is a hard judgement but contains within it some truth. By keeping the delicate balance between research and development, production, sales and, distribution, finance must be used to the best possible advantage. It must be available when and where it is most needed. Thus the accountant today, against the background of the rapid advance of technology and mechanization, is a key figure; it is no good increasing the production of anything – of products or services or a combination of both – if there is no money to increase sales: it is equally useless pouring money into research if there is none left to finance production. These are obvious, all too obvious, facts, but they are often ignored. Through an intelligent approach to management accounting – the interpretation in terms of money of the history of the recent past and the plans of an industrial or commercial unit for the coming year or years and to check whether these plans are bearing fruit in the way planned – accountants can make an immense contribution to easing management's burden. Whether accountants make good top executives is another and far wider question and an answer will be attempted in a later chapter; but it is interesting that a financial and not a technical man was, for a good many years, holding one of the top jobs in Britain – the chairmanship of I.C.I.

It is not in the scope of this book to discuss the origin of finance and how it is raised. This needs a book to itself. The assumption must be that the accountant, the financial controller, the cashier, the secretary (titles are unimportant) have been given the responsibility for ensuring that a business operation pays its way and that its results bear a reasonable relation between net profit earned and capital employed. A further assumption must also be that a board is aware of its responsibility to ensure that the shareholder's net assets earn a fair return and that they are maintained in a profit-earning condition. A company may pay its way for an unconscionable time without its management being aware of or reacting to the fact that profitability is diminishing. In fact profits may show an upward trend but the return on capital employed may be decreasing, and all too often part of this capital is undistributed profits which could have been more profitably employed by the shareholders themselves. The accountant or financial controller is the connecting link between marketing and production and board policy: he must interpret the former to the latter and convert policy into production planning and marketing budgets. The essence of the task is acceptance of the idea of planning in advance the revenue and expenditure and use of finance.

There is nothing new in this idea of budgetary control. Samuel Pepys used it when he was assigned the job of rebuilding Charles II's navy; he catalogued the Fleet, dockyard facilities, stores, and manpower requirements; he then calculated with characteristically Pepysian conscientiousness the cost of building the additional Ships of the Line needed by the Fleet. The approach that *is* new is that the budgets resulting from the agreed operational plan are made and accepted by the whole management team and become serious targets. These are yardsticks by which management's efficiency can be judged. The detailed standards used for controlling manufactured costs are based on the material, labour, and overheads needed to make the product if the available plant and manufacturing process are used in the most effective way. In the case of a purely service undertaking – for example a bank or an insurance company – the emphasis is on such factors as salaries, wages, and rents. It is in these areas that the computer's ability to process large volumes of figures at high speed finds its standard and simplest application.

The accountant's job is to play the part of coordinator; it is he who must bring together all the budgets into a Profit and Loss Statement; it is he who has the final responsibility for the production of speedy and intelligible returns. On the other hand, management must be continuously on guard against the multiplication of statements and returns for their own sake or for the glorification of the accountant producing them. Figures breed figures and their impact is rapidly diminished as they multiply; it is the accountant's task to produce to management no more statistics than are required to take effective action.

The financial controls thus evolved by the accountants in

management can only be produced if there is maximum co-operation from everyone within the business enterprise. Engineers, realizing the need of figures to show them the cost of waste and losses as well as the cost of savings that arise from improvements in technical processes and methods, must be prepared at all times to give the accountants the facts they need. Marketing men have to coordinate their efforts in a manufacturing industry with the factory and are increasingly conscious of the need for a joint sales-production programme which can only be valid if it has a sound financial basis.

Efficient management of the finance available to a business can be achieved by the introduction of many tried and proved techniques some of which will be described in greater detail later in this chapter. Production and material control, standard costing, monthly operating statements, sales budgeting, budgetary controls leading to financial planning, discounted cash flow – these procedures, varying in scope and complexity in relation to the kind of business to which they may be applied, are a sample of what management in these enlightened days realizes is essential to a proper grasp of where a business is financially heading. Of more general interest is the wider problem of the control of financial resources, and this essential control needs to be described in greater detail in this section.

Briefly it can be said that the control of capital resources is as important as the control of income and expenditure and has a direct effect on profitability. There are two reasons for this: first, that an expanding firm may well show a good profit and yet go bankrupt through lack of resources or failure to plan for its needs and, second, that unless capital resources are controlled and planned to ensure their optimum use, sales and output and therefore profits will be restricted.

Capital resources and their control are reported annually

to the owners of a company in its balance sheet. The method of presenting this report to the public and any accompanying remarks by the directors have a material effect on the relationship which exists between public companies and the world at large. This relationship may prove vital to an expanding company as it will be from the general community that the company will seek to raise additional funds.

Similarly, and at the same time, management will account to the owners on the trading results. The feeling exists all too strongly in Britain that minimum disclosure in this respect is in the best interests of the company. The nonsensical idea that turnover figures will help a competitor still persists. Prompted by the Stock Exchange rules this state of mind is changing and is being replaced by a full and detailed report of the company's trading. Increasingly, companies now include a ten-year record of their achievements, disclosing not only their overall sales analysed by product groups, but also the percentages of gross and net profit to their sales and the annual return on shareholders' funds.

Much has been written about the morality of the take-over bid. It is not necessary to generalize as to the reasons which inspire those who organize take-overs; it is probably true to say that such reasons as personal profit, prestige, and power are at least contributory incentives. It is, however, interesting to reflect that, in fact, the take-over bid has a useful function towards the investing community, especially nowadays when a larger proportion of the population are investors. The threat of these bids may sometimes prevent the directors of a company from pursuing a policy which does not give to the shareholders a reasonable return on their assest or a reasonable share of the profits. There have been, for example, many cases where the total remuneration of the directors has exceeded the total paid to shareholders or when physical assets such as properties are considerably undervalued. All in all it may be said that the expression 'take-over bid' has become something of a catch phrase which has grown up since the war and which is directly related to the undervaluation of a company's assets.

The Restrictive Practices Court and the Monopolies Commission both, in their different ways, are concerned with the problem of size and the public interest, the latter today particularly. There can be little question that too much of British industry is fragmented to the point where the public interest, especially in the matter of making exports competitive, is not adequately served. The Industrial Reorganisation Corporation is specifically charged with stimulating mergers to counter this short-coming.

*

The management of finance need not be as esoteric a subject as one might assume. To illustrate some respects of it a homely – and entirely imaginary – case history now follows.

Imagine a quite fictional Bill Smith who runs a village garage. He is successful and he decides to expand into making car trailers. He has a son, Charlie, who is a good hand as a smith and a joiner, and another son, Les, who has all the exuberance required by a salesman. The daughter Mary deals with the correspondence. The purse strings are as always looked after by Mrs Smith. Smith has a little money laid by and he uses it to buy the materials needed to make a few trailers and the family get so wrapped up in the enterprise that they put all their money into these materials. Soon there is more work than he can do and an additional man to help him has to be taken on. They find themselves, however, without enough money to complete all their trailers and sell them. Capital has, in fact, been committed too deeply without the target being able to be completed. Fortunately, however, the local squire and the doctor have faith in Smith and they put up some money. At first they are sleeping partners, but to regularize the position it is decided to form a company. The squire and the doctor are now shareholders.

The Smiths have learnt their lesson and Mrs Smith now keeps a careful eye on the use being put to the money. She has become more than an accountant, she is now in charge of finance. She brings together the ideas of her enthusiastic husband and sons and works out the plan of the number of trailers to be made and sold. Without calling it by such a name, she has adopted the modern principles of budgetary control. Charlie wants to experiment with new designs for trailers and Les feels sure that he could sell them, but Mrs Smith will have none of it; she says it is no use spending money on experiments and then not being able to pay for production. Charlie then wants to spend all the money he can get on making larger batches of trailers with more labour, but his mother points out that this is useless unless Les can sell them. She says the only way to do it is to get out a plan of the trailers they are going to produce and the dates on which Les is going to sell them. They are faced with the problem whether to try to make fifty trailers with a profit of £1 on each or ten trailers with a profit of £5 on each. Mrs Smith points out that the higher their production the more money they will need to pay for the materials and wages before they sell the product. It is Mrs Smith's job to coordinate the ideas of her sons.

Unfortunately Mrs Smith gets ill and during her illness the family get in the services of a retired bank manager who is a great man for figures. He calculates everything to the last detail and covers many pieces of paper with figures, which impresses the Smiths although they do not understand them nor do they realize that Charlie's estimates of the material and time taken in making a trailer are only guesswork and that his calculations of the work done by his paid assistants are inaccurate. The bank manager does not realize that his figures cannot be more accurate than those supplied to him from the workshop and that if he is to obtain the co-operation of each of the Smiths they must understand what he wants and why he wants it. The Smiths are still making a profit on each trailer, but as a result of the inaccurate calculations of the bank manager they again find themselves in the position of being unable to complete what they have begun and to be in danger of getting into financial difficulties. They realize that an expanding company can go bankrupt while it is still making profits. They go to their friends the squire and the doctor, who in turn approach others with a view to raising more capital to complete and sell the trailers which have been begun. The position is further complicated by the fact that the Smiths had forgotten that they must pay each year tax on the profits they earn two years before.

Fortunately the friends of the squire and the doctor have sufficient confidence in Mr Smith and more capital is found. Mrs Smith recovers her health but realizes that the work that is involved is becoming beyond her and they take on a young accountant. He is a good bookkeeper but unfortunately he is lacking in judgement and he only looks to the profits which the company is making in an increasing measure. He fails to warn the Smiths that the company must be maintained in a profit-earning condition, that it is no use making an increasing number of trailers with a diminishing profit on each trailer. The business has also ploughed back considerable profits and has paid little reward to its friends the squire and the doctor and their friends who helped the Smiths in their hour of need.

This in itself might not have mattered if it had not been that the growing prosperity and turnover of the Smiths' business has been watched with envious eyes by the very much larger company of County Trailers Ltd which operates in the neighbouring town. County Trailers Ltd see their opportunity and they offer to buy the shares from the squire and the doctor at a price which is most attractive in relation to the dividends which they have been receiving, but which is yet considerably below the accumulated assets of the Smiths' business. The squire and the doctor naturally do not wish to do anything to hurt the Smiths, but the offer is so attractive that they cannot resist it and they sell their shares. The Smiths have been eclipsed by a take-over bid.

PRODUCTION

The production function of any enterprise, be it a coal mine, motor factory, or local government, is both the deciding and the limiting factor in its conduct. The ability to produce must therefore be a major consideration when the performance, standards, and targets of the business are set.

The management of production as discussed in this chapter includes the whole function or process of manufacture, and can be said to be the science of producing the right goods in the right quantities at the right time to the right people. To achieve this impeccable objective the optimum use of men, machines, and materials must be made: to guarantee its achievement is a management task.

The management of production is not, however, an end in itself, it is a means to an end, the means whereby the ultimate arbiter, the public, is satisfied.

Every day brings an increasing need for better and more efficient management of production. Technical progress in this spectacular Space Age with the necessity for more intricate and complex designs; the need for full employment with the expanding internal economy of the U.K.; even fuller emancipation of labour; all require that production must be managed in the full sense of the word.

Thus, the management of production involves the co-ordination of the functions of Development, Design, Planning, and Manufacture. The detailed techniques by which these functions are carried out depend in the main on the

scale and type of manufacture. These can be conveniently
divided into three main categories: process production,
large-batch and mass production, and small-batch and unit
production. The chart below shows that there must inevitably be a certain amount of overlap between these types,
and that a clear-cut distinction cannot be made between
them.

So far as the detailed operations of production management are concerned, many excellent textbooks have been
devoted to this subject. The concern here is to appreciate
the management problems implicit in production and these
are described below as they affect the various stages of batch
manufacture in engineering. No apology is offered for the
detailed discussion; it is necessary for the proper understanding of the complexity and scope of the problems met in
a typical batch-production factory.

Process Production	1. Continuous flow production
	2. Process production of chemicals in batches
	3. Process production combined with the preparation of a product for sale by large-batch or mass-production methods
Large-Batch and Mass Production	4. Mass production
	5. Production of large batches
	6. Production of components in large batches subsequently assembled diversely
Small-Batch and Unit Production	7. Production of small batches
	8. Fabrication of large equipments in stages
	9. Manufacture of technically complex unit articles
	10. Manufacture of simple unit articles to customer orders

The previous section of this chapter outlined the management of finance and discussed how a business target is set. Once company policy is defined, management must work down in ever increasing detail, setting out to give instructions in sufficient detail, at the right time, to ensure that all the parts required for a given period's output are made or bought out as economically as possible; that they arrive at the right place at the right time to be tested, assembled, and dispatched to suit the sales plan. To do this requires a full appreciation and exercise of the function of production management.

As a basis, a programme is drawn up by the sales and production managers and agreed at the highest possible level, generally by the managing director or the top executive team. This is most important, since the programme settles what the company will do and the scale of its operations, indeed, it is the whole plan of campaign of the company.

Each unit for delivery must be evaluated in terms of man hours and machine hours to ensure that adequate capacity is available in every month of the year to meet the requirements. At this point, a need may be recognized for additional capacity, in which case a decision has to be made whether this will be met by working overtime, putting work out to sub-contract, or by increasing the labour force at certain periods of the year. When it is established that the load imposed by the planned output is balanced by the works capacity, the next step is to ensure that every part is ordered in sufficient time to be completed punctually. In doing this it must be remembered that although a particular job on a machine may only involve say thirty minutes actual work, the part may have to wait for several hours after arrival at the machine before it can be processed. To be confident of receiving the completed part by a certain date management must be satisfied that it will reach the machine with plenty of time for the 'queueing'. It is evident, therefore, that all the parts needed to complete a given assembly are considered and they must be ordered sufficiently long before they are required for each to take its turn in the queue. The total time that elapses before all the parts are completed is referred to as the Manufacturing Cycle, and is usually counted back from the delivery date of each unit of output. In order to make this calculation simple, it helps to divide the year into equal periods of time, say months, numbered consecutively. It will thus be necessary to order by month I all the parts required for a product which is due for delivery in month III if the manufacturing cycle is two months long.

To calculate the requirements of parts to be ordered it is usual to go back to the Manufacturing Programme and multiply the number of units of product due for delivery in the period under consideration by the number of different parts required for each unit. Certain parts may be used in more than one product, in which case clerical, punched card, or other mechanical procedures are used to combine the requirements. Some record must be kept of the orders for each individual part, with numbers received against each order, much along the lines of a stock record. It is usual to keep these manually on cards, although for large installations punched cards are more economical and a computer can be used for this purpose.

When the requirement of each part is known, the amount of material needed can be calculated and its supply arranged. For some parts, it may not be economical to calculate in such detail, and with the use of clerical effort, the quantity needed; control in such cases can be maintained by keeping a float of parts and simply replacing them as they are used. This method does not give such close control of stocks as that previously described, and there is a risk of being left with redundant stock if the usage ceases, say owing to a design change. Both these methods of stock control are used to indicate to the works' staff that further supplies of a particular part are needed, and steps must be taken to arrange this by issuing orders specifying the parts, the quantity required, and the date the parts are needed. These orders are then distributed to the various processing sections which will handle the parts through the works, and are used by the foremen of those sections to load their operators with work.

It will be seen that these procedures ensure that orders are issued at the right time for the right quantity to the right people, who can see from the Production Schedule referred to above when they must complete their work, so that if all goes well, every part is delivered on time.

Since it is the work of fallible human beings that is being discussed here, something may go wrong. So that the whole works will not be delayed for lack of a single part, a Progress Section is set up to ensure that the instructions reach the people in time, that any mistakes are rectified, losses during manufacture are made good, and that disasters are anticipated and avoided whenever possible.

The orderly flow of production is thus seen to depend on four functions: Programming, in which the amount of output per period is agreed by all concerned; Scheduling, in which the relative timetables of the various producing sections are established; Ordering, in which executive instructions are given to make and assemble specific quantities of parts; and Progressing, to make sure that everything is proceeding in accordance with the overall plan.

This account of production management has so far covered the answers to the questions all production managers must answer – How many to make? what sort? and when?

The actual details of the processes required to make and assemble the products, and the detailed specification of every part in terms of finish, machine limits etc., are laid down by departments which are not so immediately concerned with keeping to the production calendar.

The design department evolves a new design, or modification of an existing product, after consultation with the commercial department, which has established the need and the market for the particular item. The complexity of the product decides the number of stages of development through which it must go before the final stage is reached, but the ultimate product of the design department must in every case be a complete specification of the product and its performance, including a list of every part needed to make it. In the engineering world, this is usually provided by drawings of details and sub-assemblies, parts lists, and performance specifications.

With this data, the production departments take over, and decide in detail how each part is to be made. This includes laying down what machine does what operation, what tools, machine speeds, and feeds, and grades of labour should be used, and at what stages the parts should be assembled together. This is generally called Process Planning, and when orders are issued to the works as described above they will take the form of instructions to the operators to follow the process laid down.

To ensure that these instructions are followed it is usual to have a force of inspectors following the product at each stage, and ensuring that it complies with its specification.

The preceding paragraphs have set out the problems involved in the management of production of a batch-production engineering works, but similar functions can be recognized in almost every kind of manufacturing or processsing industry. For example, in chemical manufacture the first thing that must be established about a plant is its throughput capacity of processed product. This might be said to correspond to programming in batch production. The various reaction times of the successive processes through which the feed stock goes will decide the vessel capacities, pump sizes, and pipe dimensions in a way closely analogous to the scheduling in an engineering works. The valves controlling the flow of the various reagents might be likened to the clerical procedures of stock control and ordering.

The foregoing describes the main stream of actual manufacture, but there are important ancillary matters which must also be considered. For example, in the determination of the work content of the various items which must be manufactured, the technique of work study has enabled almost scientific accuracy to be achieved, so that a trained work study department is a very necessary adjunct to a manufacturing process employing labour.

The type of management decision which arises in the control of production includes extraordinarily difficult problems, in which a large number of inter-acting variables has to be considered, and the technique of Operational Research has been developed to simplify the solution of this type of problem. To take a mundane example: a computer has been used most successfully to obtain the most economical combination of the various ingredients used in cattle-cake manufacture. The effect on the total cost of marginally varying the cost of one of the ingredients can be studied, and a balanced ingredient and cost composition can thus be developed. Such a study, if carried out by normal methods, would involve many hours of laborious mathematical analysis.

The use of Operational Research techniques need not be restricted to the large process industries. Similar methods can be used as a basis for management decisions in all sizes of business.

For the process of manufacture to proceed at all, there must be premises, plant, and services and they must be maintained in good working order. The choice of a suitable site must be related to the availability of labour, materials, transport, and services, and consideration must be given to room for possible expansion, the disposal of waste products, and the provision of fire and emergency services. The selection and design of the most suitable buildings must of course be governed by the type of product and the scale of production, as indeed must be the internal layout of the building. This becomes a major management preoccupation in a plant of any size.

The maintenance of existing facilities requires careful planning to ensure that the plant is not being run down or too much money being spent in keeping it in unnecessarily good condition. The policy for plant replacement thus requires the greatest management attention. Considerable thought has been devoted in America in recent years to devising methods by which the various products competing for available capital may be ranked in order of merit – such a study has been given the glamorous name of Business Investment Analysis. As yet little study has been made in Britain of this subject, but obviously economic reasons will create an increasing need for its practice.

It is clear that business tends to expand in a series of steps as the productive capacity is increased by installing new machines or taking over new workshops. Because there is a tendency for these steps to be complex and detailed, there is a very heavy load on management at such a time, and it is often economical to employ outside assistance such as that offered by many of the large and small firms of management consultants. This could apply to the introduction of incentives based on work study; to a change of Production Control methods; to cost reduction and the provision of cost control information; and even to the provision of a new factory or department. Indeed some firms of consultants can now supply a 'package deal' which includes analysing the market, the design of a new factory, and the supervision of its construction up to the installation of the machines and the organization of management procedures necessary for a smooth flow of production. The valuable role consultants can play as a tool of management has been fully recognized

in North America and is well on the way to full recognition
in Western Europe. Absolute objectivity, a disinterested
approach, and, above all, the precious ingredient of un-
trammelled time have combined to make responsible management consultancy an important new profession.

All the foregoing has dealt with manufacturing production. This is not to imply that the effective management of
'commercial' production – banks, insurance, wholesaling,
retailing, shipping, and a host of other business activities –
is not as important. But it would be true to say that while
management principles broadly apply to any form of business enterprise, a discussion of the management of manufacturing production is more likely to be definitive. Whether
the end product is, however, a manufactured article or a
service, the production function, as was said at the start of
this section, is both a deciding and a limiting factor.

MARKETING

In the chapter 'The Business of Business' marketing, like
finance and production, was described as one of management's principal 'means'. It is a generic term which may be
broadly said to cover market research, selling, merchandising and distribution, advertising, and public relations. These
marketing functions enable business management to ascertain
accurately the requirements of actual or potential customers;
they are vital to the optimum use of the products or the
services that have been created.

Though marketing in its widest sense was described as a
central and unique management activity – no business can
flourish, much less take root, if the market requirement is
not kept constantly in view – it is valuable to analyse in some
detail the main marketing functions. But it should be said
at once that it is in the sphere of the marketing of manufactured goods – whether of a capital, semi-capital, agricul-

tural, or consumer nature – that these functions are most responsive to analysis. This is not to say that services ranging from banking, insurance, and television, to a haircut do not need to be marketed just as imaginatively, but the providers of such services – and real property should also be included here – are closer to their customers, and possibly the marketing problems are less complex.

Selection of suitable distributive outlets, wholesale, retail, or mail order for instance, is usually of fundamental importance to the successful selling of manufactured goods. The detailed problems of product transportation from the point of production to the distributor, the ultimate purchaser, or the consumer are not yet generally accepted as lying within the province of marketing and this may be explained by the fact that the producer, as represented most frequently by personnel at a farm or factory, is responsible for dispatch of the goods. In fact, transportation should be regarded as being crucial to the marketing operation.

Mechanization of agricultural and industrial production, efficient methods of transporting goods, refrigeration, higher levels of consumer awareness, and increased purchasing power have enabled the farmers and manufacturers of today to serve national and international markets. Under conditions of mass production and mass consumption, the customer, although more demanding, has become anonymous. He may be hundreds of miles from the point of production; for this reason, and because many manufactured goods must go through several stages of production, the producer and consumer are also separated in time. The car industry is typical of this situation; the time which elapses between the engagement of a Farina to produce a prototype to the purchase of the finished model in Australia, or even in the domestic market, must necessarily be considerable.

These factors mean that market research, merchandising,

advertising, and public relations have become distinct departments in many large businesses, and the post of Marketing Director – the executive whose job it is to coordinate the work of these several departments, including a selling organization headed by a sales manager – has become a feature of organization for marketing. There is also much healthy and welcome controversy raging about the position and status of a company's design staff. Thanks to the stimulus and leadership of the Council of Industrial Design and the growing awareness in British industry of the importance of good design, the design staffs in some organizations are at long last getting proper recognition and outside design consultants are being increasingly called upon. Problems of design – like marketing in the wider interpretation of its function – are common to the overall purpose of a business enterprise. The appearance and amenities of factory or office, initial product planning, the product itself, the 'face' of the firm which includes advertising and both staff and public relations; all these have design implications and as such must be accepted as a responsibility and interest of top managers.

In the small organization, and approximately ninety per cent of British businesses employ one hundred employees or less, all aspects of marketing must still be combined in the energy and enthusiasm of one individual or group. There are specialist marketing firms to advise the enterprise, large or small, which seeks objective help. There is a proliferation of advertising agencies ready to help companies where consumer choice is a social aim and, since the Second World War, an increasing number of concerns has been offering valuable specialized services in the fields of market research, public relations, and salesman training.

Manufactured consumer goods probably require the fullest application of each marketing function. Therefore the discussion from this point may be regarded as applying especially to them, though most of the principles apply in a general way to industrial goods.

*

Marketing decisions have traditionally been based on the experience, intuition, and personal observations of selling personnel, particularly of sales managers. Business is fortunate in being equipped today with an intelligence service in the shape of market research, which management can utilize for the discovery of the following:

1. Size and value of the market
2. Location and geographical extent of the market
3. Type of customer
4. Motivations and preferences of customers
5. Trends in buying habits
6. Suitable distributive channels
7. Strength of competition
8. Prices within a given trade
9. Effectiveness of advertising
10. Efficiency of salesmen and distributors

The highest purpose of market research is to ensure that the consumer can be offered what he or she wants to buy.

Management's growing use of market research proves its value, for it yields savings and profits which exceed its cost. A word of caution is, however, needed here. The role of market research has been likened to the use of Radar. It informs the users of the perils which lie ahead and it indicates the route by which mishaps may be avoided. If, before Radar was invented, a fog settled on the Straits of Dover the captain of a ship could only drop anchor until the fog had lifted; to do otherwise would have been to court collision and disaster. Market research provides management with means of obtaining information without the cost of trial and error, and it is like Radar in another respect, for its use can be most dangerous in the hands of inexperienced people. Navigators in R.A.F. Pathfinder Squadrons during the Second World War used to report how easy it was to make a mistake in establishing a Radar 'fix' of their position. While the equipment itself was infallible, an error in reading the coordinates from the set and in plotting the wrong ones on the chart could, and not infrequently did, end in disaster. This does not mean that only eminent scientists are fit to handle Radar equipment, but it does mean that a sound working knowledge of its principles is essential.

A method for collecting market information must first be selected. Because salesmen are accustomed to persuading rather than looking objectively at facts, their usefulness as collectors of information is limited. 'Desk' research, which is the collection and analysis of published material available within or outside a company, and field work in the form of observation or personal interviewing of an adequate sample are the main methods by which information is obtained. The assembled data is later tabulated and analysed.

The technique known as 'retail audit' is now practised by a number of market research firms who are specialists in this field. It involves observing regularly the stock position in a carefully selected sample of retail outlets in a specific field; for example, grocers, chemists, and confectioners. Users of this service are informed of the rate at which their competitors' products are moving off the shelves in advance of the normal indications of consumer acceptance or otherwise through the rate of incoming orders. Selling effort, advertising expenditure, and production schedules often require adjustment in the light of this valuable information.

Observing is usually neither so quick nor so cheap as questioning, but questions must not be loaded, and interviewers themselves must be unbiased. Most interviewing is conducted with the aid of questionnaires. The wording and lay-out of these is important. They should solicit all the information required, as briefly as possible. The sequence of questions is relevant, and each question must carry the same meaning to different people in order that the various results will be comparable.

Let an example be quoted: the management of a department store in a city in the Midlands was recently disappointed by the declining profitability of its restaurant, which was particularly quiet although trade in the rest of the store was as busy as usual. Customers were always offered a choice of a two- or three-course luncheon, and it was felt that business might increase if part of the restaurant was converted to a cafeteria in which snacks could be obtained. A market research organization was engaged to conduct a survey among shoppers in the store. A questionnaire was designed and a pilot survey was undertaken, but it was found at this stage that many shoppers were giving luncheon requirements similar to those that already existed in the restaurant. Upon examination this proved to be due to the particular phrasing of one of the questions 'What type of luncheon would you like?' Respondents had freely interpreted this, some giving the lunch they normally had each day at home, others listing an imagined menu regardless of price, while yet another group theorized about the lunch they thought other shoppers would like to have, disregarding their own individual wishes. A more specific re-wording of this question – 'What type of luncheon do you require in this shop today?' – limited the respondents to considering only their own lunch on that day in relation to possible factors which a day spent shopping might impose on them. An analysis of the answers which were subsequently obtained showed that most shoppers wanted quick and inexpensive snack lunches, but not served in a cafeteria. It was sufficient merely to add snacks to the menu, and when this was done business increased appreciably.

Furthermore it is essential to keep a clear head in the

matter of the interpretation of the statistics in terms of percentages that emerge from an analysis of market research in the field. A hypothetical case might be as follows: A manufacturer of branded confectionery wants to measure consumer acceptance. His sample has been carried out in a large city. The results show that sixty per cent of those interviewed prefer his brand to a competitor's product, which is roughly similar in price and quality. However, unless the respondents have been asked how much they have bought and how often over a given period, he should not be misled into thinking that his sales have necessarily been greater than his competitor's, because the forty per cent preferring the competitive product may have, on average, purchased larger quantities at more frequent intervals. This example emphasizes the paramount need for most scrupulous attention to the planning of both the questionnaire and the sample. Advertising campaigns based on a meretricious interpretation of market research are by no means rare occurrences.

Discovery of reasons for the consumer's attitude to a product may demand the use of depth interviews, sentence completion, and word-association tests. 'Respondents' are sometimes shown a series of relatively ambiguous pictures, and then explanatory stories are sought. These various techniques make up what is called 'motivation' research – the 'why' rather than the 'what' of human behaviour. The costs of such research are high because the services of trained psychologists are sometimes necessary, and because certain techniques, depth interviewing for example, require much time. People are not easily persuaded to be subjects for motivation research, and thus valid sampling is difficult to achieve. It must always be remembered by those who utilize psychological techniques that the subconscious and unconscious are not necessarily more significant than the conscious. Dr John Treasure, Chairman of the international advertising firm of J. Walter Thompson, has wisely said on this subject:

Knowing *why* people buy does not in itself solve the manufacturers' problem of what to do any more than knowing *who* buys. . . . The true 'end and purpose' of all kinds of market research is to predict what will happen to sales if a certain policy is decided upon: and, by comparison, to enable management to decide which policy or what combination of policies should be adopted to maximize sales. . . . Good research, whether concerned with behaviour or motivation, should be accompanied by a sketch of the implications of policy decisions which may be made on the basis of the research. . . .

Market research need not be a rigidly technical operation; the primary need is a resourceful and flexible approach. Emphasis may have to be changed quickly in the light of new disclosures as the research task proceeds. Thus a management may be convinced that the goods it is responsible for possess a certain limited application. It advises those who are undertaking the research of the limits to which they should confine themselves, but, as happens so often, the researchers may discover a highly promising application for the goods outside their traditional field which management has hitherto unquestionably accepted.

*

Consumers' buying habits govern the selection of distributive channels by management, but restricted resources can impose limitations; thus a small concern may merely appoint selling agents. It must be remembered that the agent and the distributor, although they are not on the payroll, are in a very real sense part of a selling organization. The number and the geographical dispersal of distributors, whether wholesale or retail, decides the size of a manufacturer's sales force.

Each salesman is typically allotted to a certain area or territory; the extent depends on the number of distributors whom he can be expected to serve, the average duration of calls, and the required frequency of calls. If many distributors are utilized throughout the United Kingdom, there may be so many salesmen that some of the sales managers' responsibilities have to be delegated to regional supervisors. Several concerns selling more than one distinct category of goods find that they can achieve more success by using two or more sales forces, each of which specializes in a particular category. This kind of sales organization is particularly convenient when each category of goods is sold to a different set of customers. However, although the characteristics of customers differ, all may purchase the full range of the company's products, in which case organization by type of customer may be desirable.

Responsibilities of sales managers vary considerably. They make significant decisions on policy in some companies but in others they are left to administer policies dictated from above. The sales manager should be concerned with the allocation of territories, the supervision, encouragement, and appraisal of sales personnel, reports on the selling operation, and liaison with other departments. He is usually based at a sales office (supervised by someone else) where statistical records of calls and orders are maintained.

Coordination of changes in policy and the solution of particular problems as they arise demand effective communication between the sales manager, the sales office, and salesmen. Sales targets must be realistic in relation to local and national market potential, and the total current productive resources of the enterprise; goodwill can be lost by delivery periods which are too lengthy.

Selection of salesmen is of primary importance. It is not

enough that a man should be neat in appearance and have a pleasant manner, in fact neither of these qualities matters particularly. But he must be genuinely interested in selling; he must be self-reliant and enterprising; he must, above all, be fascinated by people, who will assuredly respond to his interest in them whatever his surface characteristics may be. A salesman must be trained in his Company's objectives and in the product with which he is concerned, but he should never be trained to sell products or services which he feels to be bogus, for a disastrous impression of insincerity may thus be created. Equally, a salesman will never be able to do justice to his selling task by the adoption of a sales 'patter' which is inimical to his nature and personality. Because improvement in technique is always possible, training should be a continuing process. A salesman is physically separated from the concern by which he is employed, and this circumstance can lead to his identifying himself too closely with customers. He must never be allowed to forget his responsibility to the men and women in the factory; regular visits to the works, Company social gatherings, and sports events can play a certain part here.

Salesmen may be paid a straight salary, salary and commission, commission only, salary and bonus, or salary, commission, and bonus. In many industries, the traditional system of small salary and large commission is giving way to a basic salary adequate for the maintenance of a decent and progressive way of life. In sum, the Arthur Miller *Death of a Salesman* type of character, insecure, brash, opportunist, and uneducated, is on the way to becoming a British legend. And it is well this should be so.

*

Merchandising is the art of presenting goods to potential customers in the most appealing and convenient way. Marketing management has many choices in this respect. Showrooms, stands at exhibitions and trade fairs, leaflets, display cards and other material for use at the point of sale; these are some of the more tangible merchandising media.

Perhaps it is at retail level that marketing management has particularly interesting merchandising challenges, for when someone is window shopping no salesman is present to extol the merits of the goods displayed and the display itself is of high importance. A message may be conveyed by superficially irrelevant trappings. A store which sells informal clothes of a high grade may use a backdrop of posters showing lush, sub-tropical resorts, thus hoping to convey to the potential purchaser the impression that the clothes would be ideal for a summer holiday, and that, because they are fashionable and of good quality, they are customarily seen in the most exotic and expensive places. An enterprising shopkeeper in the Soho district of London, who specializes in holiday clothes, has employed a Spanish guitarist to play just inside the door of his shop between noon and 2 p.m.; this is an instance of imaginative merchandising, for it attracts people to a shop when the streets outside are likely to be more crowded than at any other time.

In the grocery trade, supermarkets and other large and small self-service stores, which are revolutionizing retail distribution, can achieve certain operational economies. They do not run delivery services, nor do they offer credit, and, most important, customers assemble their own orders. Division of labour, for example, into shelf stockers and checkers or cashiers, helps to achieve efficiency among employees, but there are no selling personnel. This absence of human contact with the customer underlines the need to use merchandising techniques. Food must be wrapped hygienically. A package should offer the customer a recognizable quantity and standard of quality, it must be attractively designed, and must link with external promotion. All food, packaged or otherwise, must be accessible, and it should be displayed in an orderly and intriguing fashion. Music is being played in some supermarkets with the object of promoting a sense of well-being and even irresponsibility among customers. In others, closed circuit television brings news of up to date promotions and prices.

There is a whisper here of Francis Bacon: 'In the declining age of a state, mechanical arts and merchandise do flourish.' Management should heed this ancient philosopher.

*

Advertising plays a substantial role in the affairs of a free society. If consumer choice is accepted as a natural corollary of such a society, if the forces of competition are to be set to work in the public interest, it must follow that the odds have to be shouted in the market-place. This is not the point at which to pursue the economic or ethical arguments which the supporters and critics of advertising advance with much eloquence. The plan fact is that unless, as in a totalitarian society, the consumer is to be given what the State alone thinks is good for him, the securing of the identification of specific products and services – 'brand recognition' as it is called – is a part of the marketing task. The responsibility that falls on the shoulders of those who hope to manage this task is a formidable one. At one end of the scale advertising can be vulgar, misleading, and inflationary; at the other, honest, interesting, and truly informative. It is a sizeable marketing dilemma, underlined by the conditions of material plenty today, to decide between these opposites – to strike a balance which, while perhaps not immediately yielding such dramatic sales results, will secure long-term advantages and sustained public goodwill. The fact that the advertising business itself – which includes the ever-increasing number of accredited advertising agencies, the growing number of advertising departments in businesses, and the powerful communications media such as commercial T.V. – accounts for the expenditure of many millions of pounds and billions of dollars, increases management's responsibility for using this potent instrument intelligently and in the public interest.

One thing is certain. The art (or craft) of advertising is an expertise and management will be wise to leave its practice in the hands of those who understand and are trained in it. Precisely because advertising touches everybody at some point or other, the work of the advertising manager or agent is often ruined by the well-meant but confusing interference of top management who, having taken a policy decision to advertise – and because this decision bears on factors other than marketing ones it must be accepted as a top management responsibility – should then leave the implementation to the experts.

*

A somewhat facile but near-descriptive phrase 'The Face of the Firm' was coined not long ago to produce the theme of an exhibition in London staged by the lively Design and Industries Association. This display sought to demonstrate how such things as print, display and production material, packaging, letterheads, invoices, delivery vans, and trade marks can, if intelligently integrated and coordinated, project the character of an enterprise in such a way as to make it readily recognizable by the public and thus form a favourable public opinion about it. Such projection, if it is necessary at all, needs to go much further; it should take care of items ranging from the design of a factory or office block to the personality and manners of the girl who answers the telephone.

Ever since public relations became a business preoccupation, a definition of this elusive operation has been sought which would enlighten a slightly bemused public who know at any rate that the P.R.O. has come to stay. A definition

comes from the Institute of Public Relations: 'The deliber-
ate, planned and sustained effort to establish and maintain
mutual understanding between an organization and its
public'; and while this may sound a shade artless, it goes
some way towards establishing what public relations is all
about, for by its very ambiguity it proves how easily a public
relations operation can be adjusted to suit about every
human circumstance. The management of a large enterprise
has, it must be said, quite new problems in this day of mass
communication, swelling ranks of shareholders and vocal
and organized labour. Straightforward advertising – a story
usually told with little subtlety but much point – is one way
of projecting a business and promoting its goods or services;
public relations is a refinement, and usually a pretty crafty
one, of this technique; it is more concerned with opinion
than sales.

If public opinion is a factor which requires the constant
attention of business management, how can management
best deal with the problem? What action should management take? There are no proper answers to this question
because the extent to which public opinion really counts has
not, and perhaps never will be, measured. Mr Earl Newsom
writes on this point:

It is generally recognized, for example, that no enterprise can hope
to achieve public confidence unless it acts in the public interest;
that is, no amount of propaganda, however clever, can make any
enterprise look better over a period of time than it really is. . . .
But what kind of actions do we mean? Every human being is far
from perfect and every enterprise even less so, if only because it
includes the activities of large numbers of human beings. And who
is able to observe the true public interest in every situation in a
contradictory and changing world? As far as that goes, who do we
mean by the phrase the 'public interest'? Is the task of human
leadership simply that of rushing to carry out the whims of the
crowd it leads? On this question current empirical data seems to

support traditional theory that the actions of leaders influence public opinion quite as much as public opinion influences the action of leaders.

This could hardly be better expressed. Though there is a note of qualified scepticism in much present-day thinking about public relations, there are management implications – indeed marketing implications – which are relevant. The public will judge a business by what it is – not by what it pretends to be. And so it is fair to conclude that a public relations operation – whether carried out by the enterprise itself, by its advertising agent, or by one of the growing number of experts organized to handle it – must start from the goal that management itself has determined and wishes to pursue in the interests of all who are affected by that determination.

*

This chapter, 'Management of What', has taken the three chief management means – finance, production, and sales – and has tried to paint a broad picture of some of the considerations that should guide the actions of the managers who are specifically concerned with one or other aspect. Apart from the fact that marketing – in the sense that a marketing outlook assures the essential dynamism of a business – is discussed in two places in this book, at the very start and in this chapter, the inference that it is hoped will be drawn is that management must see these three means as an entity, that they form a trinity of interests, and that neither one can be truly effective without a proper balancing of the other two. In any case – and in the last resort – it is the people in the enterprise who make it tick.

THE EXPORT CHALLENGE

It is doubtful whether any aspect of Britain's commercial life attracts so much cliché to itself as her export trade. Exhortations to do more of it fall with monotonous regularity from the anxious lips of spokesmen of successive governments whatever political colour. Moreover, and especially in recent years, 'economic nationalism' as a dominant force in world affairs, as well as the genuine, if overdue, attempts by Western Europe to organize her trade and politics so that a primarily European war can never again happen, have meant that clichés, as far as Britain is concerned, have a new force and a new urgency. 'Export or die' – the apotheosis of cliché – brings a wry smile to the faces of many British manufacturers, and the post-war history of Britain's export trade is littered with tombstones marking the death of the brave, but often ineffectual, efforts to inject a new approach into this most baffling of subjects. But 'export or die' is the heart of the matter so far as Britain's long-term future is concerned – a nation committed, irrevocably and permanently, to a way of life for its people which is today assumed to be what the people themselves regard as their due.

As a tailpiece to a chapter which has analysed in some detail the chief components of the managerial process – finance, production, and marketing – it seems appropriate to examine in a separate section some of the problems of exporting so far as they affect business management in Britain. The build-up and maintenance of a successful export trade involves the clearest possible understanding and utilization of those 'means' which have been discussed in the body of this chapter. Financing for export has to be seen very often as a long-term investment and something of a gamble. Export production has to be balanced against the development of the sometimes more urgent claims of domestic demand. Export marketing is more often than not a question, at the start of an export foray at any rate, of will rather than technique – of will, and indeed of luck. These are characteristics of a form of trading which is at once infinitely tedious, infinitely exciting, and infinitely important.

And it must also be remembered that Britain's overseas loyalties, more than those of all other European countries, including those behind the Iron Curtain, are inevitably split. She is not only the heart of a Commonwealth and Empire, but is also, geographically and historically, a part of Europe as well as a blood relation of North America. Critics of her anxieties over relationships with the heartening movement towards European Free Trade must remember these somewhat tormenting claims. A united Western European 'bloc', united that is to say in politics and trade, is one thing, but a united, mutually trading Commonwealth and Empire, working harmoniously with the United States, is another. Too many facile judgements have been made of what Britain should do in these matters to attempt yet another. It will be better to stick to some export management facts and leave the theorists to their never-ending argument.

In considering the question of export management the creation and service of markets must have an even greater priority than it has at home. Too much of Britain's export trade has been the result of haphazard growth. This has been stimulated to a great extent by the facts of her own historical background: dominance of the trade routes by virtue of sea power, an insatiable appetite for exploration and trading, and, above all, an ability to turn imported raw materials into serviceable and effective manufactured goods. These days are past. The world is largely explored, traditional forms of sea power have lost most of their importance in an age of jet and nuclear development, and, although the world's demand for manufactured goods is on a staggering increase as populations and standards of living rise, Britain is now up against the hard facts of tough competition. There are no longer any easy courses to take and while home demand, perpetually at the mercy of successive governments' 'stop-go' policies, is characterized by booms and slumps, it is not hard to see why such a comparatively large proportion of the export of manufactured goods from Britain is carried out by so few and such large companies. Even allowing for the fact that a far greater number of smaller firms supply essential components and thus are, in a sense, also exporters, the total effort is far below what it should be.

Is there a management answer to this recurrent question of expanding Britain's overseas trade? The answer must surely be 'yes', and the word that has again to be used, for all its vagueness, is '*will*'. Where there is a will there is a way. It is one of the most remarkable facts of Britain's export trade that in cases where a management has really had the *will* to develop overseas business – a will fortified by patriotism and a normal instinct for ultimate profit – there have been and will continue to be stories of rewarding successes. It is far more, today, a question of quantity than one of quality. The real need is for a far greater number of producers of both goods and services, as the B.B.C. would put it, to 'have a go'. Even when all is admitted about the irritating documentation, the initial cost of finding agents, setting up companies, undertaking market research and, not least, the lack of tax incentive, a thriving export trade for an island so placed must surely be to the ultimate advantage of the exporter who has thus spread his risk. And this does not even take into account the austere economic fact of the 'balance of trade' – the fact that a country importing so much of its essential food and fuel just cannot everlastingly be beholden to the rest of the world.

The question of a greater industrial rationalization, i.e. fewer, more efficient producers, raises matters which dig deep into the history and character of the British people. Size for the sake of size is not a characteristic which appeals to this still intensely individualistic community. The mergers which are going on in many industrial undertakings today may often be prompted by urgent commercial considerations, but they may also bring a considerable reaction in their wake.

One thing is clear. British export trade will only expand successfully when manufacturing and selling costs are substantially reduced; and it is inevitable that the size of the unit thus becomes a vital factor.

There are no quick answers to the question of finding export markets and going for them, but it is largely a matter of having faith in your product and going to tell people about it – again, of *will*. These considerations dominate such longer-term aspects as design and quality, for, sad to say, there is an immense amount of shoddy British merchandise to be found in the shops, the markets, and the bazaars of the world. The urgent lesson for the manufacturer who has already achieved some export trade is that design and quality are now catching up in importance as the hitherto often unsophisticated customer develops taste and judgement. Market research can teach much, but there is a melancholy lesson to be learnt from the life and death of the British Export Trade Research Organization (B.E.T.R.O.) which started in 1945 and fizzled out in 1952 after seven precarious years of existence. Perhaps the chief lesson was that facts, however accurate and compelling on paper, are no substitute for the vision and personal experience of men whose pockets are going to be directly affected by the success or failure of an export project. But some facts are better than no facts at all and the almost purblind optimism with which managements enter on an export programme, sublimely unaware of what a market requires, confident that what sells at home cannot fail to sell abroad, arrogantly convinced that instructions for use and sales promotion material produced in English will be sufficient, is proof enough that export market research is an essential first step.

Do the Export Manager and members of his department get the necessary recognition and status? In companies where there is a reasonably long history of export endeavour it is fair to say that the Export Manager – sometimes even translated to the height of Export Director – gets efficient collaboration from the rest of the management. But this is the exception which proves no rule. In far too many companies the Export Department is a poor relation strung on to a sales organization with an underpaid, overworked executive in charge, who has to stake his claim for finance for market research, travel, promotion, special packaging for overseas, and all the rest in the teeth of considerable scepticism from the Board and top management. Furthermore, he is often a man who gets little opportunity to travel and who has got to his present position through a series of accidents. Is this changing? It is doubtful whether it is. It is true that education for export is valiantly carried out by such organizations as the Institute of Export, and export courses are being put on in increasing numbers by various training establishments. The B.N.E.C. (British National Export Council) is also providing some useful stimulus. There may even be a strong case for the establishment of an Export Staff College. Recurrent pleas by harassed politicians to industry to look into export posibilities have a momentary effect, but the percentage of companies whose response becomes an enduring one is derisory, and until the craft and management of export is seen as another cliché! – a matter of life or death for the British economy – the sought-for expansion will just not happen.

Export is so often regarded as a production overspill. 'We can't get rid of the stuff here at home so let's try and sell it abroad.' This is a fatal, a negative, attitude. The Scotch whisky approach, alas! will only solve a minute part of the problem. There are of course cases where a range tried and proved on the domestic market has a prompt acceptance in a number of markets abroad, but these are exceptional conditions. A host of design, colour, packaging, technical, and servicing considerations have to be measured and catered for, and while it is true that a great number of the bigger

exporters have solved their problems by establishing production units abroad, there is still no reason why, with
adroit production planning, the necessary adjustments to
meet overseas requirements should not be incorporated into
the manufacturing plan at home. The real difficulty lies in
finding the best means of actual overseas distribution and
selling. A prodigious job has been done over the decades by
the merchant shipping and confirming houses, whose knowledge of export conditions is considerable and whose contribution to Britain's exports should never be minimized. But the
exporter should always be working towards controlling his
own exports, and whether he does this through local selling
companies, through agents whose enthusiasm and cooperation he is really prepared to encourage, or through eventual
local manufacture, are questions of timing and of product.
Timing is involved because importing conditions, duties,
restrictions, and the like, imposed by so many governments
in these uncertain political times, are often changing; the
question of the product is involved because there are still
many instances where 'Made in Britain' can be an invaluable trading asset. Even in the developing countries of the
world, where spending power is limited, too much haste in
producing goods locally can boomerang on an ambitious
manufacturer.

The previous chapter touched on the relationships between business management and the government. In this
matter of export the government can do much and, in fact,
through its Export Credits Guarantee Department, its network of officials abroad, and its energetic if somewhat
amorphous Board of Trade, a good deal of help is available
to present and potential exporters. It is always easy to criti-
cize the government, but such criticism is sterile. Much of
the blame for the inadequate understanding by British
manufacturers of the problems and possibilities of export
must be laid at the door of trade associations and the like

who – though there are shining exceptions – are so caught up in the web of petty squabbles and intrigues among their members that the real export issues become fogged –if indeed they are appreciated at all.

In a period of world-wide industrialization it may be that Britain should re-examine her entire approach to export, recognizing that she has new values to offer – values in the form of experience and know-how, of 'invisibles' such as insurance and banking, and of forms of investment which will encourage ultimate trade in the types of capital and semi-capital equipment for the quality of which she is justly respected and for which she has already built up an impressive export total. This section is concluded by a short case history of the growth in export sales by a remarkable firm called Dexion which, at the time of writing, has 'gone public' and which began by specializing in slotted angle. They are now world leaders in storage. In the end it is, as has been stressed, a question of will. A management that contains within it a real determination to trade abroad will succeed whatever the difficulties.

Dexion Limited are manufacturers of the Dexion Slotted Angle system (now known all over the world). Like most good ideas, Dexion is essentially simple. It consists of a range of steel angles perforated in such a way as to facilitate the construction of rigid, bolted frameworks. It can be used to build not only storage installations varying from a simple rack to a vast, three tier structure, but also – as Dexion discovered when they exploited this remarkable product to the full – building frameworks, grandstands, Olympic scoreboards and radio masts. It has a thousand uses.

Such a versatile product clearly offered a challenge from the point of view of the export market. No market was too small – every market could use it. The first Dexion was produced in 1948 and in order to get an allocation of steel, then rationed by the Government, the company had to accept a 100% export target. In the home market at that time only aluminium Dexion was available. This fact probably had a lot to do with the company's attitude to exports – overseas countries, however small, had to be tackled aggressively and a sales organization specifically developed for this purpose. Export sales were not just a spill-over from the home market but were negotiated and developed for their own sake. The growth was rapid. In the first five years exports rose at an annual average rate of 140%. Today, in spite of the fact that the total number of markets is smaller than ever owing to overseas manufacture of the product and, in some cases, import restrictions, nearly 50% of the output of Dexion's Hemel Hempstead plant goes overseas.

Dexion have built up a worldwide network of enthusiastic and co-operative distributors. This cost a great deal of time and money, but the results have made it very worth while. From the first, it was company policy to visit all major markets at least twice a year to check on distributor performance, to train their salesmen and to play a positive part in selling to governments and the eager commercial organizations. Distributors who fell short of the required standards were replaced as quickly as possible: it is vitally important in the export business that distributors should be capable of exploiting the market to the full.

In certain important markets, highly trained Dexion men are stationed permanently, either joining the distributor's staff or remaining company employees. In many cases costs are shared by the distributor. Another important step was the setting up of subsidiary sales companies in, for example, Germany and the U.S.A., so that the company could maintain better control over marketing policy and build up substantial additions to the already high export turnover.

Dexion is always striving to improve its standards of technical sales promotional assistance to distributors and overseas companies and to develop new methods of sales promotion. A vital factor here is the importance it attaches to marketing. Marketing is the intelligence – the brain – which provides a constant source of up-to-date information to the sales and promotional teams. Modern marketing techniques spotlight opportunities for business that might otherwise be missed. The whole distribution network is examined regularly and improvements made where necessary; distributors' performances are assessed in the light of accurate market research and adverse trends are corrected in good time. Overseas markets are changing markets – what is acceptable today may well not be tomorrow, as new factors appear which make the need for change imperative. Dexion is never afraid to try something new, something bold in their export marketing. Although Dexion does not want to profit by other people's misfortunes, disasters such as earthquakes and hurricanes are inevitable. Dexion angle is invaluable in such tragic situations for the emergency housing of the homeless and the improvisation of canteens and casualty stations. When disasters of this kind occur, a Dexion man from London is usually on the spot very quickly, working with charitable organizations and government relief agencies.

Dexion have always made it their policy to improve their products, technical 'know-how' and service. That is why the first simple uses for Dexion angle have now developed into a wide range of structures. Given the necessary technical expertise, it is logical to progress from, for example, a light duty storage rack to a two or three tier installation, to the design of a grandstand. That is why, at so many of the public ceremonies of the newly independent African states, including Ghana, Sierra Leone, Tanzania, Uganda and Kenya, the grandstands were built of Dexion Slotted Angle. Other important grandstand contracts include Guyana Independence, the South East Asian Games and the Rio de Janeiro Carnival, 1968. Similarly, the principle of the rigid and bolted Dexion framework can be applied to a wide range of structures – from a simple workbench to a 60' span building.

For many years, Dexion's policy was to keep the U.K. and export operations separate, but with the growing sophistication of the storage market in so many countries abroad as well as in the U.K., it was decided to integrate them so that there should be a complete cross-fertilization of marketing and selling techniques. A great deal of training is done on all levels both of distributors and Dexion staff. For the former there is a series of correspondence courses in selling and design implemented by field training by visiting Regional Sales Managers. For the latter, the courses include sales letter writing, shipping techniques, finance and credit control, selling and marketing. Management training plays an important part. After all, the drive and impetus of the company's export comes largely from the individual managers, so no effort is spared in giving them every opportunity of self-development.

Perhaps the most important factor in Dexion's success is good staff selection. That a company is only as good as its staff is a maxim taken seriously by the company. No expense is spared in a constant endeavour to attract the right kind of recruit into the company.

What emerges from all this is a picture of a bold and enterprising marketing policy. Companies cannot afford to wait for overseas opportunities to present themselves – they must seek them out and in some cases make them. Dexion salesmen carry their company's message to the farthest corners of the world, from Japan to Canada and from Iceland to South Africa, but they would be the first to admit that they could not achieve the results they do, were they not supported by an aggressive marketing sales promotion and product development organization at home.

7

Family Firms

THE vast proportion of business enterprises, old and new, has its origin in the family: the skilled tradesman or the inspired innovator flowering into a sizeable family firm and ending up as a public company is a familiar pattern. This progression may take centuries or it may be achieved in a short span of years. Whatever the pace the family firm today presents a unique set of management situations.

A definition must be sought. Perhaps the most satisfactory would be, simply, to describe a family firm as one which is predominantly owned and managed by a family. Whether the firm is a private company or a public one, the founder, or the founder's descendants, still exercise control.

There immediately arises the question of size. It is clear that very different management considerations arise in the case of a British company like Cadbury Bros Ltd (which has recently joined forces with Schweppes) employing many thousands of people – a business keenly interested in its family responsibilities – from those in a small engineering works employing three hundred people and run by a father and son. If management's aim is to secure a high degree of work satisfaction for its employees, in addition to good trading results (in any case the two should go hand in hand), the size of the operation presents different problems.

This matter of work satisfaction depends to quite an extent on size, and the larger the firm the more difficult it is to achieve that sense of sharing and belonging among employees which is today accepted both as a basic psychological need and vital to effective management. A large family-owned firm is in much the same position as a business of corporate ownership; its management has a plain duty to employees to ensure that the job is worth doing, and it usually has the resources to carry out what is required, always provided that the requirements are measured and understood. Because of its size, it is forced to use a good deal of professional management.

But there are less and less large family-owned businesses left in existence today. Taxation, death duties, and rationalization have brought about the reorganizations of many firms which, a generation back, were distinguished by men of immense prestige and personality. Austin, Morris, Leverhulme, Melchett and Dewar are now the names of shadowy figures who have been replaced by forbidding intials like D.C.L. and I.C.I. or manufactured words like Unilever. The trend, though melancholy, is inevitable in modern conditions.

It is, however, in the galaxy of middle- and small-sized businesses that there is still a great number of predominantly family-owned firms which have been sustained by the prudent counsel of legal and taxation advisers, and which are protected from the worst depredations of the Inland Revenue.

It would seem that the family owners have to make a serious decision. Will they accept the management responsibility, generation by generation, and see it through themselves, or do they see their role as benign heads of the concern, showing themselves as occasion demands, supplying an often welcome form of benevolence and paternalism and leaving the management to experts?

In the first case – the acceptance of management responsibility by the family owners – there is little question but that the quality of management tends to become diluted as generation succeeds generation. Except in rare cases the fine fervour which typified the founder's approach to the development of the firm, a fervour which was often compounded of inventive genius and idealism and which was underwritten by an ardent desire to make money, has evaporated. The graveyards of commerce and industry are full of the tombstones of businesses which have perished in this way or which have lost precious and valued identity through amalgamations and mergers. And yet there is often to be found a persistent belief in many families that, by some almost divine right, theirs is the obligation to go on leading, long after the urge or the incentive and the capacity to lead have gone. Sons feel they must show their fathers, even though their characters and tastes are utterly dissimilar, that they can 'pull it off' and that they can do every bit as well. There are, in fact, deep complicated psychological forces at work here which are too seldom given proper consideration. An interesting and recurring example is of the succession to an autocratic family leader by two sons. There are occasions when such a succession works well because the two brothers complement each other: one has the father's tough character; the other brings more humane standards to bear. As a combination it can be highly successful. The problem usually arises with the generation after that: cousins don't so often get on together!

But when a family firm is just holding its own, though signs of decay are not hard to see, there are different problems from the employees' point of view. It has so frequently been stated in this book that, financial rewards apart, responsible participation is vital to a worker's satisfaction and there can be no question that access to a boss who is easily identifiable, who carries with him something of the history and the 'ethos' of a firm, is an important consideration. This is particularly true of women employees, who respond to paternalism however remote it may be. But if there is no efficiency, if the owner is simply there because he feels he ought to be, without having thought through whether or not he has the proper qualifications, it is pretty certain that the employees will soon become disenchanted. Management, it cannot be said too often, implies leadership; it is almost asking too much to expect that every generation in a family will supply a leader.

There are outstanding exceptions to these rules. In the brewery business in Britain, to take but one from many possible examples, there are notable cases of generation succeeding generation and making an admirable job of it. The point to note here, however, is that in such instances not only has the fullest training been given to young Mr Tom (or Dick or Harry) when he entered the firm, but he must have made it clear to himself and his colleagues that business is a career that he seeks and he must bring to his eventual management tasks a thorough knowledge of what he is doing. There are no short cuts because, when there are, directors and managers who get (or should one say, inherit?) their positions without competition invariably and naturally arouse the resentment of other able and ambitious employees who want a chance to get to the board room. It is essential for family management in such circumstances to avoid being surrounded by the second-rate.

The second approach raises quite different questions. This is the decision, by succeeding generations in a family firm which is well and truly established, to act as benevolent figureheads leaving the management to professionals.

It calls for a very special kind of discipline, once this decision is taken, to avoid interfering with the management under these circumstances. 'After all,' the argument runs, 'I own the business so why the devil shouldn't I chivvy my management, keep them on their toes!', and so on. This can be a fatal attitude. An owner must feel free to ask questions and be kept briefed about what is going on, but if he nags and bullies he is breaking faith. This is often reflected in the creation of a certain type of manager who, with his 'anything for peace' philosophy, turns into a pale version of what a manager should be. The debt that is owed to the founder of a successful family business by succeeding generations is often best paid by the acceptance of one prime responsibility, that of finding the efficient managers and then placing utmost confidence in them. And the acceptance of that responsibility can in itself be a complete justification for enjoying without guilt the fruits of the founder's efforts.

A part-time, member-of-the-family chairman with wide outside interests in, for example, charitable or cultural fields can be a sheet-anchor to a busy management. With the wisdom and detachment that comes from a wider view of life such a man or men can very often bring to management a fresh approach which, if management is wise, it will do well to study.

This can be a two-way affair. In these days of shifting and uncertain loyalties there is much to be said for managements making the very most of family tradition and reputation in a business. It implies no loss of prestige or power when a non-family general manager or managing director adroitly uses the family representatives in the best interests of the firm's development and as a means of giving employees a sense of belonging to something more defined than an impersonal machine. Paternalism needs, however, to be carefully and wisely handled. A chairman's letter to a man who has done thirty years' service can be a valuable and welcome aid to management, whereas the granting of a loan to someone in the typing pool in a branch office to meet an urgent need should be within the competence of the man on the spot. The danger lies in too great an emphasis on the 'family' as the fount of *all* wisdom and generosity.

Most of the foregoing applies to middle- and large-sized family-owned firms. There is still the host of small businesses which account for a great part of Britain's industrial and commercial effort, and which in so many instances derive their stimulus and lead from family management. In fact

ninety per cent of British firms employ 100 people or less
and the family element in such enterprises must still be pre-
dominant.

The twin questions of continuity of management and the
general well-being of the employee largely resolve themselves, in the case of such enterprises, to the state of trade.
Full employment destroys the smaller family firms that un-
derpay employees or give them impossible working conditions; the market will absorb them elsewhere. So far as the
succession is concerned, when it is not a question of almost
traditional behaviour – 'what's been good enough for Dad
will be good enough for me' – better education and wider
opportunities tend to attract the brighter people away from
the often restrictive family business atmosphere where short-
age of finance excludes a reasonable rate of expansion.
Despite all these difficulties, the family business pattern,
especially in small enterprises, will take a long time to dis-
appear: alert, enthusiastic, able family leadership is still
very important to industrial and commercial progress.

*

There is one additional factor about which it is hard to write
precisely but which must be touched upon and which will be
better illustrated by a case history.

Many family firms are jealous of their reputation in what
may be termed the fields of design, craftsmanship, and service. Against considerable odds such firms, expanding because the world's desire for better-designed, better-made
things is expanding, have to hold on tenaciously to their
high principles of quality and design and to the craftsmen to
maintain them. In these circumstances it is probable that the
family-business atmosphere is the most conducive to the
maintenance of these standards. The business of Heal's, a
quality shop in London, an independent family business for
over 150 years, is a good example. Here the first principles

of quality and design are maintained because, so to say, succeeding generations of the Heal family are imbued with a sense of responsibility. There is no question but that men and women working in such an atmosphere derive a special sort of satisfaction from the family tradition.

It may well be that a family firm which places quality and reputation above all else will not make the same profits as a competitor less concerned with the imponderables of design and craftsmanship, but this is an instance – and let such instances be praised – when profit is not the whole story. It may also well be that such firms are particularly vulnerable to take-over bids, but here again there are many instances of considerable family courage in the face of mounting temptation.

In sum it may be said that there is plenty of room for family businesses so long as the family representatives can bring either management skill or benevolence – or both – adjusted in each case to the character and requirements of the situation. If these qualities are not forthcoming the rest of the management will have a hopeless task.

The story of the famous pottery firm of Wedgwood is so relevant to this particular aspect of family leadership that it now follows.

*

The Wedgwood story is not one of *unremitting* success, and yet, despite many vicissitudes, this firm, which was founded in 1759, has steadily increased in prosperity and size, and today its name ranks with some of the world's biggest producers in terms of public recognition.

Josiah Wedgwood started the business when he was twenty-nine with a capital of a few pounds in a factory which he rented for £10 a year. He had only a rudimentary education. When he died thirty-six years later he left a fortune estimated at a quarter of a million. His wares had become famous throughout the old world and the new, and he had established British pottery as an industry of international importance. Not only this: he had become a Fellow of the Royal Society and had gained no mean reputation as a social (e.g. abolition of slavery) and economic (e.g. construction of canals) reformer.

Josiah's business was not one that sprang from the industrial revolution. Although he evolved a number of new techniques, there were no radical changes in the processes of manufacture, but he showed a flair for management which was far beyond his time. He rationalized the arrangement of his craftsmen's workshops, interspersing them with ovens and kilns, and organized the whole into a coherent productive unit. He introduced reforms in conditions of employment which gave his work-people much greater security than had ever before been enjoyed in the industry. He was probably the first industrialist to see the importance of marrying art with industry, and he employed many well-known artists. He was also an excellent designer and craftsman in his own right. His standards of taste, quality, and integrity were extremely high.

It is doubtful whether – with the exception of the manager of his London showroom – he ever enjoyed the services of competent managers, although for eleven years he drew great support from his friend and partner, Thomas Bentley. After Bentley's death Josiah engaged Alexander Chisholm as his secretary and 'chemistry assistant'. William Hackwood acted as a kind of technical manager, but Josiah must have done a prodigious amount of executive work himself. He showed a great flair for salesmanship and promotion, and a keen sense of public relations which even today pays dividends to his successors. Although in his letters to Bentley there is abundant evidence of his shrewdness, he appears to have been remarkably unpreoccupied with financial matters. He seems to have got on to good terms with many influen-

tial people – including the Queen – not apparently because
of his rapidly growing personal wealth, of which there was
very little sign outside his home at Etruria, but largely – and
simply – because he made very good pots indeed and took
subtle pains to let people know that he did so, and that it
was not difficult to obtain them.

His health was never good – at the age of thirty-eight he
had his right leg amputated – but in spite of this he was
never content to rest on his laurels, always seeking improved
processes, new clay bodies, fresh talent for his studies, or
new ideas for promoting his wares. By the time of his death
he had established a Wedgwood tradition: one feels he
would have showed little surprise had he been told that his
business would still be flourishing – indeed would have
greatly expanded – in two hundred years' time.

But this was not his only legacy; he and his wife, Sarah –
who was also his cousin – were to have many talented des-
cendents, including Charles Darwin FRS, and the late Ralph
Vaughan Williams OM – to name only two out of about six
hundred! None of them *had* to earn their living making pots,
but each generation seemed to have had a sense of responsibility about the business. It had to go on.

Josiah was succeeded as head of the business by his second
son, Josiah II, who lived until 1843. He did not have his
father's knack of getting on well with all and sundry but
must have been an interesting man. William Blake, the poet
and painter, did catalogue illustrations for him, Samuel
Coleridge (to whom for many years he paid a 'pension') was
a devoted friend, and it is doubtful whether Charles Darwin
would ever have gone on the *Beagle* if his uncle Josiah had
not intervened on his behalf. But Josiah's comparative lack
of interest in salesmanship and promotion, combined with
the trade depression following the Napoleonic Wars, had
long-term effects on the fortunes of the business. Nevertheless he stuck to his post with, one feels, considerable stoicism,

and he made his mark on the production side. While Josiah I had organized the works, Josiah II began to mechanize them. He installed a steam engine to drive the mill, the clay mixers, and possibly some of the pottery machinery. But his most important contribution was in the realms of labour relations. Just as his father anticipated the demands of his customers, so Josiah II seemed to anticipate the demands of labour. Although his friends considered him austere, he was well liked by his employees (they subscribed to his election expenses when he stood for Parliament) and treated them with more than customary consideration for his day. Indeed the industrial explosions of the nineteenth – or if it comes to that, the twentieth – centuries never seem to have hit the Wedgwood factory, where in its whole history there has never been a strike.

As a business, however, Wedgwood declined in the time of Josiah II. In the 1830s the London showrooms were closed and many valuable records and moulds were sold or destroyed. Shortly after his death his executors sold nearly all of the first Josiah's country estate and village, retaining only the seven acres on which the works stood. This was an error of judgement, although it may have been dictated by financial necessity. For the purchaser of the neighbouring land was a coal and iron company whose growth and operations were destined within the next sixty years to cause serious mining subsidences and deposit of iron dust and dirt that cost the business many times the sale price of the land.

Circumstances such as these must have tempted the next generation to drop the business. It was in fact taken over by the second Josiah's third son, Francis, whose real interests seem to have lain with men like Kossuth and John Stuart Mill, rather than the making of pots, but who nevertheless proved himself a manager of great stature. There was more mechanization – scientific labour-saving devices were introduced, a filter press for drying clay, blungers for mixing, and pug mills for preparing it for the potters. Several coloured clay bodies, still popular today, were introduced.

The taste of the sixties and seventies was mediocre and demanded great elaboration, which was not in the rather austere and elegant Wedgwood tradition. In the realm of design, therefore, Francis had to break new ground, and although most of his products conformed to the taste of his day, he was responsible for one particularly interesting experiment – that of employing the artist Emile Lessore, in 1858. By this time the artist and the potting craftsmen were drifting apart and aesthetic standards suffered accordingly. Lessore, however, painted directly on to specially thrown pieces. Francis perhaps had that almost uncanny Wedgwood instinct for anticipating trends to come. For although Lessore's contribution made only a negligible difference to the firm's turnover, his appointment ante-dated by only three years the formation of William Morris's company of artist-craftsmen, the date which is usually taken as marking the modern conception of applied industrial design.

Francis was a radical – he is reputed to have bought land in different parts of the country in order to have more votes to support the great Reform Bill – and he was responsible for considerable advances in labour relations during this critical period of the growth of the trade unions and factory legislation. He controlled the business from 1843 to 1870; during that time it flourished and the number of workpeople increased from about 400 to 700.

The rest of the century was a period of hanging on. The fourth generation was not very successful and it was left to the fifth, which entered from about 1903, to start tackling the problem of modernizing the works. Cecil and Frank Wedgwood worked devotedly – for many years without even a salary. The high costs of outmoded machinery and the intricate hand processes which were still necessary to produce the desired standard of quality were having a serious effect on the home market, and the First World War put an end to the hitherto important export trade to Europe.

In 1906 Kennard Wedgwood went to New York, and opened a small branch office, which was to manage the sole selling agency for the U.S.A. It must be remembered that all this, and the modernization of the factory, was being carried out with very little capital, and that from 1895, when the firm was incorporated as a private limited company, until 1917 no dividend was paid on either the ordinary or the preference shares. Kennard showed the usual degree of Wedgwood devotion and within five years his agency was making a profit and in 1920 it was incorporated as an American Company.

Kennard was later joined by Hensleigh, who in the 1930s literally 'carpet bagged' round Canada, building up a business connexion which resulted in a separate selling company for Canada being set up in 1950 in Toronto. Virtually the whole of the capital of both the Canadian and the American companies is owned by the parent company.

The sixth generation of Wedgwoods had a much more professional attitude than their predecessors. The late Josiah, (Managing Director from 1930 and Chairman from 1947 to 1967) joined at the age of thirty in 1928; Clement Tom, who was Director in charge of building, John Hamilton, now Deputy Chairman, and Hensleigh Cecil (until recently President of the New York Company) all joined around the same time. All were under thirty. The slump in the early thirties was to prove a great testing time for their managerial qualities.

Josiah was a trained economist, and almost immediately had to plunge into the grim business of cutting out much of the 'dead wood' which the company at that time was carrying. It is typical, however, that rather than wholesale dismissals, which were the general pattern of the day, at Wedgwood people were pensioned off and the existing *ex gratia* pension scheme was greatly extended. But more important, and with considerable courage, the work of modernizing the factory and its management was pushed forward with great vigour. Improved systems of costing and stock control, loss records, and sales and order analyses were started, and an interesting experiment in bulk production (for Cadbury's) at a very low profit margin did much to keep the wheels turning and to counteract the devastation of the American market in 1933. By 1934 this generation of Wedgwoods had miraculously managed to pay an ordinary dividend, and in 1935 the company made better profits than ever before since it became a limited company in 1895.

Next came the great act of faith. The directors decided to abandon the Etruria factory and build a new one in the countryside of Barlaston, six miles south of Stoke-on-Trent. Money had to be raised, and considering the insecurity of the times the Wedgwoods seem to have had remarkably little difficulty in getting it. Shares were not floated on the open market, but £200,000 was raised by debentures, £50,000 by a further issue of ordinary shares mainly to members of the family, and a further £50,000 out of liquid reserves. With this comparatively slender sum plans were made to build the most modern and efficient pottery in the country, if not in the world. But two years of planning, surveying, and negotiating brought the directors to September 1938 and it must have required great courage to go ahead with their plan at such an inauspicious time. While Mr Chamberlain was waving his piece of paper at Heston airport, the foundations were being laid at Barlaston, and by August 1940 the main part of the building was complete. Two-thirds of the employees were transferred to it, the remainder continuing at Etruria until the end of the war when there was a further expansion of both factory and capital and the transfer was completed.

The highly organized Barlaston factory called for a much

'tighter' quality of management. In 1946 Norman Wilson was appointed a director – the first non-family member of the Board for fifty years. He had been Works Manager for many years and had played a vital part in developing the new factory. In 1946 F. Maitland Wright was also appointed to the Board. He had previously been a director of another pottery firm and was connected to the family by marriage. But for some time the directors had been watching problems of management with particular care and today most of their managers are under the age of fifty, some having grown up within the firm – or at least the industry – but a number having received professional training and experience in other fields. Titles like Cost Accountant, Order Progress Manager, Work Study and Training Manager, and Personnel Manager were virtually unknown in the pottery industry, but they are a vital part of the management structure in Wedgwood, and have helped to increase productivity by seventy-five per cent in twenty years.

Good labour relations have an important bearing on the quality of pottery production, which, at all stages, still calls for a high degree of hand craftsmanship. Wedgwood were one of the first firms to set up a Whitley Council, and their present Works Committee carries out its welfare and management advisory functions smoothly but vigorously. There is a contributory pension scheme for male employees and a superannuation scheme for all members of the staff, a generous sick pay scheme, and a profit-sharing arrangement for staff and key workers. This has all contributed to the *esprit de corps* which is self-evident to the 35,000 visitors to the Barlaston factory each year, and to the record of long service on the part of many Wedgwood employees.

Such developments as these have been matched on the Marketing side by the innovation of Wedgwood Rooms – shops within shops – staffed, designed, and operated by the firm, under concessions from nearly forty stores throughout the country. This has been of immense importance because, prior to this development, and with the exception of the firm's showrooms in London, New York, Toronto, and Sydney, the Wedgwood displayed to the public was left to the choice of individual store buyers. Wedgwood's own retail organization has provided direct contact with the public which will probably be used increasingly for purposes of market research. Sales in the home market have been increased 2700% since 1938 (before adjustment by price index). Concurrently with this development, the firm also set up its own public relations and advertising department. This was another innovation calling for outside personnel.

With this high degree of organization taking place the Wedgwoods may well have been tempted by the mass market. But this, of course, would have meant discarding their greatest inheritance, often described as the 'living tradition' of Wedgwood. In fact from the 1930s onwards the directors placed far more emphasis on good industrial design and quality than ever before since the first Josiah's death. Indeed it is not surprising to learn that the present Josiah was Chairman of the Royal College of Art, was closely associated with the Council of Industrial Design, and was one of the keenest advocates of the Design Centre. In 1934 the directors appointed a graduate of the Royal College of Art as their Design Director, and today they have a total of four such graduates on their design staff. In addition they have employed a number of outside designers, such as Arnold Machin, Eric Ravilious, Edward Bawden, Richard Guyatt, Robert Goodden, and Laurence Whistler.

In 1963, for the first time in Wedgwood history, a managing director from outside the family was appointed. The new executive head of the firm was Mr Arthur Bryan who had joined Wedgwood fifteen years earlier as a management trainee.

Under Arthur Bryan's leadership, Wedgwood has made

in four years some of the biggest strides in its long history. Within two years of taking the helm, Arthur Bryan was planning unprecedented moves for Wedgwood in the take-over business. The first was in January, 1966, when the old-established earthenware company of William Adams (founded in 1657) was acquired. Three months later, Wedgwood had purchased Tuscan China Holdings (which included the famous fine china houses of Royal Tuscan and Susie Cooper) and in July 1967 a fourth famous name was absorbed by the Wedgwood Group – that of Coalport China (founded in 1750).

Another major step was taken in May, 1967, when the company was introduced to the London Stock Exchange. For the first time, the public had an opportunity of investing in the Wedgwood business. Although very few shares appeared on the market in the first twelve months, they proved to be much in demand and the price soon showed a considerable increase. The City was undoubtedly impressed not only by Wedgwood's success of past centuries but by the last ten years up to 1967 during which time the company had achieved record results annually – profits up from £150,000 to £640,000 in 1966. Return on capital over the same period had improved from 9% to 25%.

And further expansion was continuing, for it was announced in 1966 that a factory extension would be built, costing £800,000, which would increase productive capacity by one-third when completed in 1969. Export sales had reached 70% of total production (Wedgwood was among the inaugural winners of the Queen's Award to Industry in 1966) and the call for greater output was vital to keep pace with incoming orders both from at home and abroad. Even though there had been impressive increases in productivity (output per person raised by 40% in eleven years up to 1967) this had not coped with the extra demands (the volume of sales was up by 70% in the same period). So in

1966 Wedgwood decided to introduce more mechanization wherever possible in manufacturing processes and at the same time started to use a computer bureau to ensure the optimum use of productive resources, and to gain other benefits from improved costing, ordering and despatch procedures. These advantages would also be enjoyed by the subsidiary factories in the Wedgwood Group, which by this time employed 3,500 people.

The beginning of 1968 heralded another important event for Wedgwood. The late Josiah Wedgwood relinquished, for health reasons, his position as Chairman and Arthur Bryan took on his role – again the first man outside the Wedgwood family to hold the post. He was joined in his responsibilities as Managing Director by Peter Williams, F.C.A., who had previously been company secretary and finance director. Josiah accepted an honorary life presidency.

After nearly 210 years' trading, Wedgwood is poised to enter the toughest but perhaps the most lucrative and exciting period of its history – led by highly professional management with many new ideas for increasing the company's share of the market and with an enthusiastic and vigorous approach to its problems.

In a chapter entitled 'Family Firms' the study of Wedgwood's provides an almost classic example of the synthesis of family tradition with professionalism in management. It is worth recording the late Josiah Wedgwood's reply when asked to say what was the most important thing about a family business. He smiled a little wryly: 'It has its own special problems, but it makes you take a long-term view'.

8

Getting the Best from People

THE reader who is expecting to find in this chapter a treasury of information on such subjects as work study or incentives will be disappointed. Those management techniques which are being used in ever greater varieties to get that valuable extra ounce or two ('motivating to maximum productivity' might be another way of putting it) from workers are heavily documented and less than justice would be done to them were an attempt made to compress into a few paragraphs, matters which are the subject of a considerable literature. The role that work study, for example, can play in the management of production has been discussed in an earlier chapter. It is just worth noting that this particular technique tends to be associated in most people's minds with manufacturing production rather than other forms of human activity; the hoary old symbol, the stop watch, tends to be seen only in relation to men and women who are working machines whereas, in fact, there is scarcely a single activity which is not susceptible to the kind of detached, clinical examination which work study provides. What about the average manager's average day? What about the indecisions, the 'puttings off', the surreptitious peeps at a newspaper, the gossip, and the intrigues? What sort of a picture would emerge of a manager's day if as conscientious a study of his or her movements were made as those which are applied to manual or clerical workers? It would often be a very surprising picture indeed.

But the sort of person a manager needs to be, the objectives for which he is managing, and some of the ways in which he should organize for securing the objectives, have been discussed earlier in this book. If the manager is guilty of mis-management of his own time in the strictly 'scientific' sense there is no reason to suppose he is the worse manager for that. As this book has repeatedly stressed, qualities of a less tangible, less measurable kind are needed from the manager who is truly worthy of the name.

The unanswered question – and possibly the most difficult to answer – is 'Can, in fact, management make people work better' or 'How can management get the best from people?' This question must be faced. If management is to make the best of its main resource, the human one, it must think hard and long about the resource. Accepting that people work because they have to – and usually want to – management must try to evolve ways and means of making work something more than mechanized drudgery, uninspired and uninspiring routine, or just sheer boredom.

Four factors need to be tackled at the start of this discussion. The first is to dispose of a myth. A great deal of current management thinking and organization, especially in relation to the tasks given to 'personnel' and 'human relations' departments in large firms, rests on the assumption that workers need to be sold on the idea of work – that work is somehow inimical to the great majority of mankind and that therefore there is a responsibility on these specialists to take over what management itself should be doing. Are these assumptions true? Most people surely want to work – work satisfies a psychological necessity; people also want to work because they want to eat, although it should be said that the Welfare State removes some of the pressure in this direction. And the point is that a man works best at what he can do best. That must be a manager's firm belief if the best is, indeed, to be obtained. It is, after all, a reasonable assumption that managers themselves have reached management level because managing is what they like to do – what they feel they can do best. The unwilling manager, the man who has accepted responsibility reluctantly, is in most cases a pretty useless leader. This point is returned to later in this chapter. The second factor is the question of the relation of work to pay. Pay is a primary necessity because pay ensures the opportunity to live a life outside work which satisfies those desires which are fundamental to most mortals – to eat, to sleep, to love, and to cultivate their gardens. But how many managements realize that there is a big difference between the way workers and managements regard the wages a business enterprise can afford to pay? To management the wages bill is a part of the business cost and, as such, must be flexible and capable of expansion and contraction in the light of trading conditions. To the worker his wage is his income, his livelihood, and as such needs to be a stable element. It is the basis upon which rests the whole of his private, intensely personal destiny. Although this book is not about economics it must be stated here that the conflict between management's and workers' views on wages – the difference between flexibility and stability (complicated by the social objective of full employment) will be unlikely to be resolved by the trade union cry of a 'guaranteed annual wage' – a cry which sounds well enough when conditions are good but which is hollow in times of depression. Management's task here is inescapable; it is to evolve wages and employment plans for workers which take note of all the predictable elements of a business's development.

While writing of the relation of work to pay – the second factor under consideration in the matter of getting the best from people – a word must be said again about profits. Profit is necessary for business survival. Do workers understand this? Is there not still a strong hostility to the idea of profit in most labour forces – a hostility which has been inflamed by the loose talk of politicians? The making of profit is still regarded by many as a form of 'worker exploitation' and all sorts of ingenious devices have been thought out by managements to drive home to workers what profit is really about – profit-sharing schemes, share-ownership arrangements and the like. The Fairfield Shipyard experiment was an instance where the management set out to explain to the workers the meaning of profit and the effect of their actions upon it: the future of the company and their very employment depended on the workers' comprehension and acceptance of the principles involved. Unfortunately, the company was absorbed into a group before the results could be seen. But it is fair to say of these efforts that usually they are only partially successful: the resistance is still there and is possibly only beginning to yield now that, in Britain, at least, rising living standards have made profitable free enterprise suddenly respectable: headline news in fact. The old conception of profit as being somehow outside and beyond the worker's comprehension – an objective which was subject to dark and impersonal forces – is slowly disappearing but a sideways glance at most nationalized industries is depressing enough. Here is total State ownership but nobody would claim that workers in, for example, the coal mines of Britain are particularly 'motivated' by the desire to make them profitable though in fairness to both managements and workers in these industries nobody yet seems to have established objective criteria for their working. Should they make a profit they are accused of exploiting a monopoly; should they make losses they are said to be wasting public money!

The third factor which has to be examined briefly before some answers are attempted is the question of fear – fear of not being in work and thus of the corroding indignity of unemployment. In Britain the combination of higher living standards and full and reasonably stable employment has meant that society has accepted an obligation which has virtually laid the ghosts of the thirties. Management can no longer wield the weapon of fear any more than workers need to be haunted by it. That this work motivation has been practically eliminated is one of the great social achievements of this century although it can be said that the long memory of workers must keep governments and managements for ever on the alert. But, paradoxically, not only have new fears been substituted – fear of boredom and fear of the atomic bomb – but a vacuum has been created for management to fill. That the fear of unemployment (and the derisory 'benefit' that went with it) has disappeared does not automatically spur workers into frenzies of better work, ambition, and involvement. New motivations must fill the vacuum – motivations which take care of the new and challenging era that lies ahead.

A fourth factor is the pervasive problem of the re-training and re-deployment of labour. As a result of technological change, some industries become less labour-intensive and, indeed, obsolete. Areas of the U.K. where, traditionally, son has followed father in a certain skill cease to require that kind of worker and he becomes genuinely redundant. It is a long and difficult task to persuade people to pull up their roots and go elsewhere or, if they wish to remain in familiar surroundings, to be prepared to re-train in order to work in new enterprises set up precisely to meet technological requirements. Allied to this trend is the narrowing of the gap between skilled and unskilled workers. The craft unions are anxious to maintain their pay differential and their exclusive right to certain types of work, but there are many opposing forces at work – three examples are management's need for flexibility of labour, the increase in new technologies and cost rationalization techniques such as job evaluation. The anxiety comes to the surface not only in disputes with management but also with other unions. The shipbuilding industry has been particularly troubled in this way; and witness in the railway context the dying A.S.L.E.F. fighting for survival with the N.U.R.

Factors which have been discussed as an essential preliminary to what this chapter is trying to find out should be repeated. First: people want to work but whether they can be made (or even want to) work better remains to be examined. Second: there is a basic difference – possibly an essential difference – between wages as expressed in terms of cost and wages as expressed in terms of income. To highlight this difference may be to acknowledge, contrary to what many wishful thinkers may say, that managements and workers have not got identical goals. To describe this situation as being 'on different sides of the fence' and to suggest that the lack of identical goals means an 'unbridgeable gulf', and all the rest of it is emotional rubbish. But it does indicate that management has to re-think its relationship to those who are managed. Put another way: management's clear duty is to lower costs in the name of efficiency and development – overall costs, that is to say, of which the wage content is a part. It is the workers' interest to get higher wages. These interests though different are not opposed, for if there is no business there is no work for anyone.

One other point must be made, of a general kind. Everyone in the business enterprise is, or should be, a worker. In any case, as the introduction pointed out, a vast majority in business today are employees. Words are tricky things. The distinction in this chapter between managers and managed has to be made because the consideration is whether management can make people work better, but it is not intended to draw a picture of a cadre of able, devoted, hard-working men and women destined to manage millions of reluctant lazy work-people. The manager as much as the managed is the victim of normal human imperfection.

*

What then are the motivations upon which managements must base their managing if workers are to give of their best? There are many approaches to this fascinating problem, some of which are factual and some others philosophical. Given that a stable wages policy meets a worker's first motivation for work (remembering that he wants to work anyway), that of ensuring enough money to underwrite his independence and individuality outside working hours and to give an opportunity to improve his social position and status, the structure of the wage must be such that there is full awareness of the job to be done, its value to the enterprise, and the degree of responsibility attached to it – above all to the capacities and talents of the man or woman carrying it out. That is really the contribution of work study to management practice. 'Scientific Management' – an intimidating phrase – is simply the scientific study of work. It analyses it into basic elements and seeks to improve the worker's performance in each of the elements. Another somewhat lengthier definition is: 'The systematic, objective and critical examination of all the factors which govern the operational efficiency of any specific activity in order to improve it.'

There is much controversy today about work study and a sizeable literature on the subject. Clearly, with the new technologies being brought about by automation, controversy will rage the more shrilly in the future. The point is that work study in its least controversial aspect recognizes a basic fact which is that work needs to be thoroughly studied if the worker, who is a human being, is to be given the best chance to fulfil himself. Whether the worker is confined to carrying out individual operations or whether he or she does better doing the *whole* job alone or in a team is a refinement of a question too large to be discussed.* The fact remains that a

---

*It is, however, relevant to note here that people generally want the companionship – indeed the respect – of other people and therefore working in an acceptable group is more often than not an important motivation. A manager must take care, however, to see that real potential talent is not lost in the more immediate attraction and security of the group.

big revolution in management practice took place when human work was looked at systematically. Today it has been shown that work study applies to every form of industrial activity – the design office, the bank, and the insurance company no less than the brewery or the engineering plant. 'Activity sampling' as it is called in the more rarified atmosphere of the laboratory or drawing office can lead to as much improvement as method study and work measurement in a production shop. Information – standard information that is – on methods and times for carrying out, in the best way, repetitive operations are of great benefit in ensuring not only some technical procedures but provide a firm and equitable basis on which incentive payments can be made where management and unions are in mutual agreement.

It might be well here to make a distinction between motivation and incentive. The two are different. An incentive is something that someone offers to someone else. A motivation is within a person: it is very often an irrational, inexplicable impulse or instinct. A worker is motivated to work better for reasons that do not necessarily stem from incentives handed to him from outside. Indeed one of the puzzling subjects facing management is the fact that higher productivity very often comes from workers receiving relatively low rewards from management and who, it must be assumed, are motivated by considerations of which pay is but one element. This is not to say that pay, except in a tiny minority, is not still the priority. It is arguable, however, whether a person's motivation for productivity will be changed by a wholly money incentive and especially today when most basic material needs are being satisfied.

*

Is it not becoming increasingly clear that management has got to think about those motivations which are harder to define and which are susceptible to the influence of leader-

ship and planning rather than the incentive of money –
motivations which alone will give that valuable extra ounce
or two? What are management's responsibilities in these
directions? Can it be assumed that pay and job security,
important in themselves are, indeed, 'musts' in any situation, are any longer sufficient to give the worker that sense
of responsible participation in a business enterprise to which
this book has referred in earlier chapters?

Responsible participation: these are two very significant
words in the context of this chapter. Has not the great fault
of management in the past been a pre-occupation with organizing repetitive jobs for workers which are in no way related to the wider concept of the total business operation;
which, so to say, isolate the worker completely from the
management picture so that he or she has next to no idea
what the total object of the exercise really is? Peter Drucker
gives a telling example which may be quoted here:

A mail-order plant recently organized the handling of customer
letters. Till then the work was organized by individual motions.
One clerk answered complaint letters, another one inquiries, a
third correspondence on instalment credit, and so forth. Each only
handled what could be answered by printed form letters; the few
letters that required individual handling or judgement she passed
on to the supervisor. Now each clerk handles all correspondence
whose names begin with the letter 'a', for instance. Nine hundred
and ninety-eight out of every thousand letters still are answered by
form letter. And there the work itself is fully engineered, as fully
pre-determined, as fully laid out – and as repetitive – as before.
But instead of repeating one particular motion again and again,
each clerk now handles the entire range of motions – thirty-nine to
be precise – involved in routine relations with the mail-order customer. And while that rare letter that requires judgement is still
not answered by the completely unskilled clerk, she is supposed to
write out her suggestion how to deal with it before handing it to
her supervisor. As a result productivity has gone up about thirty
per cent; turnover of clerks has dropped by two-thirds.

This case merits much thought – remember that Elton Mayo in his famous Hawthorne experiments showed that it was not necessarily the reorganization alone that increased output. It is a classic example of organizing human beings, as Drucker puts it, 'for peak performance' because essentially it recognizes that most people want to be part of a whole, that it is no longer sufficient to expect that the best work will come when the worker is isolated, when he or she is without status and information. Or perhaps that is putting the cart before the horse: possibly the way this should be expressed is that management has got to concentrate its creativity on making certain that the worker participation *is* responsible, for it is doubtful that, unless management thinks this way, workers will ever give that plus which is the difference between work and better work. As with every other management problem there are exceptions. But these exceptions do not prove a rule. Unhappy, isolated workers – so the researchers into human relations say – sometimes produce the best output. This may be, but as Alan Fox, the Oxford industrial sociologist, says, in reviewing progress in this field: 'the problem of people and productivity is far more complex than any of the generalized conceptions . . . solutions which lean on authority, control and scientific rationality in the planning of work no more have the universal answer than do solutions which look to high morale, consultative management and building challenge and autonomy into the job. Each type of solution works well in some situations and badly in others. We need to train some specialist managers with the skills to tell one situation from the other.' The Fulton Report on the Civil Service, published in the summer of 1968, is relevant. It pleads for a less 'amateur', a more professional, approach to running our country.

*

And so the area beyond financial reward is approached – the area in which the ordinary worker has somehow got to be made to feel responsible and involved – the area in which the workers' motivation goes beyond the immediacies of incentives offered to him with almost cynical detachment. Whether workers want responsibility and involvement or not is beside the point; managers have got to create that want in much the same way as they have to create a market.

The first essential in organizing human resources so that a better job will be responsibly done is to make sure that workers are doing the jobs that they can do best in an environment which is friendly and informative. It is often said that a general sense of satisfaction among workers – a liking for the company, approval of its working conditions, belief in the merchandise or services the company is producing – is not enough. This is true. A worker needs more than a vague sense of contentment. He needs, let it be repeated, to feel that he is participating responsibly, whether alone or in a group, in an enterprise the overall objects of which he can understand, and the surest way to achieve that object is to see that he fits into the right place and that he is doing a job rather than performing a movement. The one exception here may be women workers who, their minds usually being full of subjects out and beyond their chore, are conceivably happier doing repetitive work: even this is, however, arguable.

This puts a particular selection burden on 'middle management' (as it is often called) – the foremen and supervisors who are closest to the workers and who are best situated to measure the capacities of those around them. It will make selection the more important as new machines take over more and more of the repetitive work hitherto carried out by people, thus throwing up the need, to take one example, for maintenance, repair, and control personnel who will have to exercise considerable responsibility.

A second essential raises the controversial question of standards of output. Much of present-day thinking about greater output is related to setting standards and rewarding those who exceed them – the 'Stakhanovite' principle in fact. There is room for much argument here, and once again it has to be said apologetically that the subject demands a book on its own. But it cannot be overlooked entirely when getting the best from people is being discussed. There is the school of thought which claims that workers themselves should set their work 'norms' – that when management sets output standards they are inevitably low because they are based on an average, and that the workers who exceed them become disaffected either because they tend to despise management's complacency in the matter or because they don't want to let the side down. Another school argues that imposing an example from above, which is another way of describing an aspect of leadership, implies setting high standards whether of work or behaviour. The question is whether managers, clear about their objectives, are prepared by their own example to make the standards worthwhile ones.

The implication here is fortunately clear for managers even though it is obscurer for workers. To get a high standard of performance from workers, managers have got to perform highly themselves. They must, as a previous chapter explained, plan ahead, give out instructions loud and clear, inform, and, above all, avoid delays and hold-ups – they must, in sum, manage. By so doing, by behaving completely responsibly themselves, managers will, it is hoped, transmit a sense of responsibility to those they are managing. Techniques for increasing productivity with financial rewards as a basis and playing fields, canteens, and 'music while you work' as ancillaries are, then, not enough. Motivations that are within workers themselves are likely to yield the most effective results. A worker must feel responsible for what he is doing, for in accepting that responsibility he accepts a challenge. The French say, with typical wisdom, that '*l'appétit vient en mangeant*'. So it is with responsibility. The more one has the more, generally, one wants. This raises the larger matter of promotion. Management is often guilty of a blinkered attitude to encouraging promotion from the lower levels. It may be that this question should be looked at downwards and upwards, so to speak; downwards in the sense that promotional opportunities are a clear responsibility for the creative talents of managers; upwards in the sense that the 'responsibility-acceptor' will find a new motivation for doing better when he has tasted a little of the satisfaction that accepting responsibility can bring.

There is another aspect of getting the best from people which successful managements today are wisely proclaiming as a recipe for success in this field. That is the question of change. It has been said a good many times in this book that a manager must always be driving towards the expansion of his business or the improvement of the operation he is managing. Innovation and change – not just for their own sake but logically applied to development – are essential ingredients of business progress. But such growth means that there will be ever more changes – new ideas, new machines, new methods, and, sometimes, new faces. Workers respond instantly to being taken into a manager's confidence, whereas rumour, the story only half told or not told at all, can be disruptive and unsettling. This is something managers often forget. It is a matter of communicating, and this is as much a management quality as it is a management method.

Professor E. W. Bakke at Yale, considering an aspect of worker motivation – or, rather, worker satisfaction – defines a responsibility of management as being to ensure that the worker 'understands the forces and factors at work in *his* world': forces and factors which are often to do with change. This is not the same thing as taking the broad view on economic and political matters as top manager, whose horizons have, of necessity, to be wider, The sort of information that top management transmits, from, so to speak, 'on high' is often totally irrelevant, indeed far beyond the comprehension of average workers at both lower management and payroll level. And even if it can be comprehended it is often useless information at the level at which the work is done. Thomas Fassam, former Chief Work Study Officer at I.C.I., has an original thought in this connexion. He suggests that British industry should use its 'not inconsiderable influence on the daily and weekly press and on TV, which do the job of mass media communication with little conscience but great efficiency, because they have access to the minds of people in their leisure time and thus can easily overwhelm the education efforts that even the giant organizations can afford.' When Professor Bakke speaks of '*his* world' he means the immediate environment of people. Works or Staff Councils – not on the complex plane of management/union joint consultation, but of a more domestic nature – can do much good. Such joint consultation can, however, only be effective if managers have the ability to see that meetings are properly and efficiently conducted, that chairmen are briefed, and that the elected delegates are given every possible help so that their 'reporting-back' to their constituents will be constructive. Above all an atmosphere must be created which is really conducive to the cut and thrust of uninhibited argument.

But it is also more than that. Workers, if they are to be made to feel responsible, must share the whole business adventure and feel that it is worthwhile. It is no good treating a labour force like a lot of sheep. Change is both exciting and disturbing; exciting because it is a huge stimulus, disturbing because latent in most people is an apprehensiveness about the unknown and the unexpected. The worker who can go home at night and say to his wife that he has been consulted about changes that are being contemplated – even that his advice is being sought on the best ways these changes should be planned – is already sensing something of the real dimensions of responsibility. And it should be added here that all too often the truly forgotten people are the white-collared workers. Except in a few cases they are not organized and their sense of frustration and isolation is immense. The payroll worker is today a good deal better off.

'Getting the best from people' was perhaps too ambitious a title for this chapter. There are precious few management 'rules' and, certainly, when dealing with an issue as dependent on human issues as this one, any dogmatizing on the subject would be – and rightly – suspect. The future of business, with ever-developing new technologies, is heavy with challenge for management. Quite a different sort of 'best' is going to be required from both tomorrow's managers and managed.

*

It would be disingenuous in a book about management – and especially in the context of getting the best from people – to leave aside any consideration of management's relations with the Trade Unions. Unions – the 'fifth estate of the realm' as Churchill has called them – for all the T.U.C.'s air of resolute bewilderment (typified perhaps in the expression on the face of the Epstein figure outside the T.U.C. Headquarters) have become an integral part of Britain's industrial pattern. As such it is the job of managers to work with, rather than against them. Today the unions have a vested interest in both sustained prosperity and good management. They might even be described as cooperating with management – a revolution in union thinking since the War.

The reason for this revolution in union thinking is full employment. Workers can hardly be expected to be enthusiastic about new and labour-saving machinery or techniques when there is more than marginal unemployment.

Nowadays their leaders – or at least the Trades Union Congress – can afford to be enlightened and forward looking. The T.U.C. have a Production Department which works devoutly to push trade unionists through appreciation courses in work study and who, in turn, 'sell' the idea to the rank and file.

The report of an early post-war Union study group's visit to the U.S.A. reflects the way in which attitudes developed. It was something of an historic event because, in support of a recommendation that the larger unions should establish production engineering departments and train production engineers, the team agreed:

Where Management are progressive and seeking to use 'scientific management' techniques in a reasonable manner to step up production, unions should be prepared to cooperate. If managements try to be aggressive the need for effective trade union action is accentuated – not to the point of resisting new development but to see that abuses are eliminated and that the inaccuracies of 'scientific management' are not exploited at the expense of workpeople. When managements are not sufficiently enterprising and progressive, are unwilling to step up efficiency or extend markets through lower prices, then unions must press them to do so.

It should be added here that the T.U.C. in publishing the team's report did not commit itself to the acceptance of all its views and recommendations. But of course in recent years attitudes have changed. It is most significant that the T.U.C. has been able on a majority verdict to support a government incomes policy which limited wage increases and insisted on improved productivity in exchange for cash. The problems involved in containing the dissident unions and the militant section of the rank and file are enormous. Positions gained after years of devoted effort are not surrendered without a struggle and the relation of pay to performance is an idea inimical to some.

The depending involvement of government in wages and productivity bargaining has focussed public attention on the successes and failures of the modern management-union encounters. The public have frequently borne the discomfort created by these skirmishes which have caused untold damage to the concerns involved – witness British Rail and B.O.A.C. One of the more successful of the new generation of agreements was that signed by the management and unions of British Oxygen in 1966. The initiative in this instance was taken by the unions representing 4,500 transport drivers and process workers in the Company's Gases Division, which consisted of 55 different plants and depots. The unions wanted higher basic rates, a shorter working week and a revised wage structure. They were convinced that with modern methods, better organization and more flexible working practices, the existing work could be completed in very much less time. The company agreed and engaged a firm of management consultants to assist in creating the framework for an agreement. After some months of method study and work measurement a target of a 15% reduction in working hours was set, while earnings and output were to be maintained. Methods of reducing hours varied from plant to plant but with greater flexibility and cooperation much was achieved: for example, a two-shift day system on some loading bays: the ending of demarcation between fillers and loaders of cylinders: and the raising of the operational speed for all vehicles to 30 m.p.h. The implementation of the final agreement took place as planned. Average hours of work were reduced from 52 to 44: average earnings were maintained: and there was no increase in the wages bill and no reduction in output. In addition a firm base for future development of these principles was established to the benefit of both the workers and the company.

The nationalized industries have long been concerned with improving productivity, but have not always been blessed with peaceful or financially successful results. At British Rail, Lord Robertson set in motion in cooperation with the unions 'planned productivity' which increased efficiency but at the same time retained a full understanding of the human problems of redundancy and re-training. Regrettably, British Rail's imputed inefficiency is still an expensive national joke despite the Beeching axe and other costly weapons. More heartening is the profitable performance of the National Coal Board over a period when on the one hand its market is shrinking and, on the other, more and more pits are becoming highly automated. But even in this industry it is the human resource which is retarding progress. It is a measure of the latent potential that productivity has increased steadily, despite absenteeism and the continuing drain in manpower. The bare statistics leave little of the N.C.B. story to the imagination: post-war pressures pushed coal output upwards, but in 1967 output was 10% lower than in 1947 and manpower employed was 400,000 compared with 700,000: output a manshift increased about 60% over the twenty years, but nearly all of this was achieved between 1957 and 1967; the percentage of mechanized output rose from almost nil in 1947 to nearly 90% in 1967, while the number of active collieries decreased from 950 to 450. Two hard facts governed the course of the industry over these years, firstly, the competition from other fuels and secondly, the necessity to develop machinery to exploit the full potential of the mines. Iron age methods and the attitudes and organization that went with them, lacking the profit incentive, had to be transformed into a slim, modern, competitive business. The most up-to-date machinery and the most up-to-date management techniques are now accepted by the majority of the industry's work-force. One of the first productivity agreements to meet the criteria specified by the National Board for Prices and Incomes, which covered wages and conditions at the ultra-modern

Bevercotes Colliery, was signed in January 1967. Piecework in the industry is a thing of the past. Many thousands of miners have been transferred from unprofitable pits to profitable ones: for a large number this meant moving home. Many more have been re-trained and absorbed into other industries. That all this has been achieved, although not altogether painlessly, is a great credit to unions and management.

*

Figures must be approached with caution, but it was estimated in 1967 that the total working population of Great Britain was somewhere around 24,000,000. There were 15,000,000 male workers and 9,000,000 female. Manufacturing industries accounted for one-third of the total. 10,000,000 were members of 574 unions (there were 1,323 unions in 1900) of which 170 were affiliated to the T.U.C. T.U.C. membership represented nine-tenths of the total union membership.

What is formally called 'Industrial Relations' has, then, become an important preoccupation for management and especially management–union relations. The chief characteristic of these relations until recent times has been the industry-wide bargaining covering practically the whole of the manufacturing section of the economy. This had a curious effect. It meant that while Ministers of Labour and Union Leaders assumed the proportions of royalty and film stars so far as press coverage and, indeed, public interest were concerned, management at the domestic level became impatient of the shop steward and the Unions severely restricted his responsibilities and authority. Only in a few instances – in the iron and steel industry, coal and some sections of engineering – did management see its role as the task of working out a suitable relationship with union representatives 'on site'. This unreal split between national and domestic bargaining has now come to be recognized as a major defect in the system of British industrial relations. The national agreements are the cause of nation-wide cost inflation because they are used merely as a platform from which the bidding starts locally. Lord Donovan's Royal Commission report on the Trade Unions devoted many paragraphs to this problem. The result has been that the new management approach to workers, particularly unionized labour, is to improve its relationship by means of more direct management – employee communication as distinct from management–union procedures which are, in any case, so often conditioned by national considerations and nationally recognized personalities. The kind of joint consultation through Works or Staff Committees or Councils, discussed earlier in this chapter, are management's attempts, usually sincere, to humanize industrial relations in a local way; the personal function has become an important managerial activity and is a specialist operation in many businesses. For all the obvious reservations and criticisms it attracts to itself, personnel management (there are 9,000 members today of the Institute of Personnel Management) will grow as business complexity grows. It could be argued that, at this point in a discussion about trade unions, the question of irresponsible behaviour by labour and its representatives should be tackled. Unofficial strikes disgrace the industrial scene and make nonsense of the laboriously built, all-too-fragile fabric of labour relations. One of the greatest difficulties is that many 'wild-cats' are carried out by unofficial action groups over whom the unions have no power. The dockers and building trade workers have produced examples of this industrial anarchy in recent years. Nobody, however, not even Donovan, has been able to suggest a solution acceptable to all parties. It is not so much that the prospect of legally enforceable contracts frightens people, but that it is impossible to draft a law to enforce registration of all contracts.

Business cannot divorce itself from such happenings. Sufficient to say that the unions as much as management need to do a good deal of urgent thinking on the subject. One of the truly disappointing facts of the last decade has been the unions' seeming reluctance to press ahead with speed and purpose in the matter of putting their own house in order. Whatever a Royal Commission may or may not recommend, the *will* to adapt the trade union structure to the pressure of the second half of the twentieth century must derive from union leaders themselves.

9

The Development of Managers

'YOU can't train managers! They're born, not made!'
Twenty years ago, this remark was sure to have been made
at some stage of any discussion about the possibility of
management training. It did indeed represent the general
view held in business. The provision of the men who were
eventually to take responsibility for the management of an
enterprise was regarded as a matter of making sure that
enough young men entered business at the foot of the ladder.
When the need arose, those who became managers were the
people who had best survived the struggle up the rungs to
the top. Character was the best help up the ladder and
character was the main qualification for management. Experience they must have also but they would gather plenty
of this on the way up.

Even hindsight does not justify finding serious fault with
this recipe: two parts character and one of experience. Was
not British industry nourished by it in its swift rise from the
cottage looms of the seventeenth century to the mills and
workshops of the nineteenth? The men who covered Britain
in a network of canals and railways, who took the infant
sciences of electricity, heat engines, and chemistry and
developed them into great industries had no management
courses or executive development programmes, but they
seemed to manage very well without!

And yet today the development of managers is one of the
liveliest topics of discussion. Management courses and schools
thrive and multiply; many large companies, encouraged by
the Industrial Training Act, have their training departments
and even those who don't at least pay management training

the compliment of feeling guilty about it. Nor is this a quirk of the British character: the rest of Europe is equally involved, while America is an exciting and even bewildering pullulation of education theories and practice.

This evidence of effort and interest need not be taken as unquestionable proof that the conscious organized development of managers is in fact necessary. The hard-headed businessman who never puts money into anything without good reason is as much a myth as Economic Man or Freudian Man; businessmen are as adept as are artists and poets at chasing the will-of-the-wisp. And yet there are many current developments that command attention and show that it is more than just another management fashion. It has lasted longer than most fashions, and indeed is becoming sturdier every year. It has withstood the critical onslaught of many jealous disciplines from outside industry, and has now established the ability to take them into alliance and adapt them to its purposes.

*

To understand why business, which has developed so successfully for so many decades, should need organized education for its managers one needs to look at the changes in business itself, rather than any special values or discoveries in the nature and practice of training. In fact, present theory on development of managers is less different from the time-honoured patterns than one would suppose.

The main changes in business during this century are in scale, complexity, and technical skill. This is repeating what has been written earlier in this book, but must be reiterated in the context of development. The traditional theme in the evolution of an enterprise has been the family firm with a limited number of employees and operating relatively simple processes, in a world of *laissez faire*. Managers received an admirable if unconscious training which started the day they were born. They soaked up the atmosphere of business round the family breakfast table; they studied the practice of management from the example their grandfathers and fathers set; they were given responsibility in business in the same natural stages as they were given it for the conduct of the rest of their lives. Today, however, in size alone many businesses have far outgrown the capacity of any family to supply managers: although the small firms are more numerous, the large ones employ a growing share of the total industrial workers. They set the pace and provide the foundations for the small firms.

Business – and this has also been already stressed – has also become more complex in its relations with the rest of the life of the community. Its size and complexity have altered the pattern of internal relationships and communications. It is more closely geared financially and by legislation to the needs and policies of central governments, of local authorities, and of other countries and international organizations. Lastly, business has developed its techniques and increased its power so that ever more skilful and flexible methods of control are essential.

In these altered circumstances character and experience are no longer sufficient. Effort and opportunity to learn and understand the total business situation are required; methods of developing the coming managers must be evolved, and it is the evolution of such methods that is so important and interesting in the field of management development today.

*

In spite of this growing recognition of the need for the nurturing of potential managers, there are seen all too frequently the horrid instances of businesses which have neglected to consider how the future management is to be provided. Firms who lose a key man through an air crash or motor accident, or whose senior executives have grown old together and are due to retire within the next few years, with no replacements ready; or firms who face the slow loss of markets through the lack of the energy and imagination of younger men in the managers' offices; these have all neglected to cultivate their own garden and must bargain in the open market place for the management talent they need. Their cries for help are to be seen in the 'tombstones' in the Sunday newspapers and the emergence of 'management selection' experts whose job is to find staff. These consultants have the sole object of unearthing suitable men and women for the more senior posts that industry is finding it increasingly difficult to fill from inside. (Management Selection Limited might be described as the pioneers of this work in Great Britain). Their approach to the job is a systematic and careful analysis of the job and its background. Not least they study the personalities with whom the new appointee will have to work, a vital assessment indeed.

The functions of the service are not always clearly understood. It does not try to relieve managers of the responsibility for choosing their staff, but to give them skilled assistance in this task. Its main values are to give top managers a chance to get an informed and detached view on the appointment and the relationships involved, to provide specialized facilities, to recruit possible candidates, and to bring an experienced judgement to bear at the selection stage. The final responsibility, however, always lies with the employer.

It is the traditional role of the consultant, comparable with the services available in other urgent fields. The advice is directed to ensuring that there really is a square hole and the fitting of a square peg into it – all too rare a thing.

Although one purpose of management development is to make possible the introduction of new methods and techniques, the primary need is to provide for the succession. As the present managers retire, leave, or are promoted to higher levels, there must be men with suitable training and experience from whom selection can be made to fill the vacancies as they occur. It may be right that vacancies should sometimes be filled from outside, for new men will bring in the stimulus of new ideas and different standards, but it is risky, expensive, and disappointing to the existing staff to be forced to look outside as a panic measure. How strange to be enunciating such seemingly obvious truths! But how seldom are they grasped. A form of Micawberism in the matter of management succession – 'somebody will turn up' – is all too prevalent.

A full development policy will therefore start with the recruitment of young men of the right calibre, for unless the essentials of character, intelligence, and personality are present at the start, no subsequent training can develop them. Careful thought should be given to the number of potential managers who should be recruited. It should be realized that wastage of staff by voluntary leaving, or by the inexorable statistics of death and sickness over the thirty years from ages twenty-five to fifty-five, has been as high as seventy per cent; even if the upheavals and slaughter of wars are eliminated in the future it will still be necessary to provide about three times as many recruits at the entry into the pipeline as need to emerge at the management end twenty or thirty years later. This estimate of the right number to recruit is not easy to fix. Over-provision is expensive and causes disappointment to those who cannot be promoted.

This book has emphasized strongly that there is a continuous gradation in the scope of management responsibilities, from foreman or first-line supervisor up to the top policy-making group and down again. There is no point in the chain at which it can be said that the function of management ceases. Management responsibility in varying degree and scope exists at all levels down to first level supervision, including the heads of staff departments who are not in the direct chain, and training must provide for the development of men to fill all such positions.

This catholic definition of the managerial function greatly simplifies another problem – that of choosing the men who are to be the future managers. If it is restricted to mean top executives only, and if only those intended to reach such a level are designated for development, money will have to be put on certain horses long before they can have shown by their performances what their true form is likely to be. There is also the danger of disheartening those who are not designated. Finally, life is made much harder for the 'crown princes' themselves. Many a junior executive has been picked from among his fellows and sent away to some famous training establishment to learn the art of management, or has been given some carefully designed scheme of job rotation and has found as a result that his superiors suspect him, his colleagues resent him, and that he takes years to become acceptable again. It is far better that the development schemes should take every man involved in the work of management as far up the rungs of the ladder as he can climb, and as far as there are vacancies to fill.

This approach will also help in the difficult matter of 'talent spotting'. Particularly in larger firms, and in the absence of very careful searching by senior executives, young men with potential for management may be blushing unseen, and this potential may go undeveloped while the firm is screaming for outside talent in the advertising columns of the press. The wide net of a comprehensive development scheme will help the locating of such men by its careful appraisal and study of those undergoing training.

*

How then should a company make the most of its management resources? What are the best ways of discovering and developing men of the right calibre? The Robbins Report considered that 'education for management as such is a subject of considerable complexity, and opinion is divided on what methods of training are proper'. It is fair to say that opinions are still divided but the divisions are not as great as they were and some general principles are emerging.

It is healthy that there should be many different approaches to the problem. No one standard method can be expected to fit the conditions of all businesses or to satisfy the needs of all levels of managers. The history of management development is very short and the period of experimentation is far from over.

In commenting on the short history of the interest shown by business in the training of managers, it is foolish to pretend that no large organizations have existed in the past without studying and in some way solving the problem of training its future leaders: the problem has faced man since his settlement into agricultural civilizations made large organizations possible. The student of management literature might well start with Plato and Aristotle! The armed forces, the civil services, and the great religious organizations have all evolved their particular solutions to the problem, and business can look at their solutions with profit. But the purposes of these other organizations are very different from those of business, which must work out its own methods.

Business methods have to take into account not only the individual, but also the organization in which he operates and the external environment. The relevance of these three considerations has been discussed in earlier chapters and now assumes special significance. The old ideas of solely internal, on the job development are outdated, as Lord Franks discovered early in his inquiries into business education. Introduction to the total business situation and instruction in an entirely professional approach are what is required today.

The most radical changes in the business situation have been brought about by the advance in scientific knowledge in recent years. Perhaps the computer is the main banner under which this advance has been made. The computer has been much misused, but it is now passing through its 'number crunching' days towards the goal of the total information system. In its train it has brought a host of mathematical techniques: its analytical powers have opened new fields for research.

Sociology, psychology, cybernetics, ergonomics, autonomics and many other futuristic disciplines play their part in today's business. All these are tools to be put to the best use by today's managers in the conduct of business in an increasingly complex environment. Competition in the market place will get fiercer, market patterns will continually alter and governments will interfere with legislation and persuasion on an increasing scale. Within the large corporations, as bureaucratic tendencies increase with size, Northcote Parkinson's famous laws will further test the abilities of management. Speed of action, personality and effective communication will have to be injected into the lumbering giants.

It is thus inevitable that amateur managers can no longer be tolerated and professionalism must be the cry. And this is not a problem to be left entirely to the individual. Self development has its part to play, but the development of men, the fourth and perhaps most important resource of a business, cannot be left to chance. Being fundamental to the successful future of a business the policy for the development of managers should be in the hands of the board of directors. In addition the programme will not bear fruit unless the board give it their full support and keep it under continuous review.

A management development programme might include the following ingredients:

1. A long, hard look at the present organization structure to ensure that it is logical and effective.
2. A projection of the structure into the future to assess managerial needs as the company alters in size or character.
3. Creation of job specifications.
4. A register of existing managers together with their career history and an appraisal of performance and potential.
5. A succession plan and recruitment policy.
6. A management by objectives programme.
7. Internal training plans.
8. External training plans.

The final three ingredients, being more controversial than the others, deserve some comment.

The concept of the Executive Development Programme, as the Americans call it, is by no means new. It has been around in one form or another for many years in America, but has not been so popular in the United Kingdom. Even the Americans were beginning to admit that E.D.P's were not the panacea they had hoped for. The real stumbling block was the method of management appraisal. A subordinate was appraised by his superior against a set of characteristics such as leadership, initiative, reliability, judgement, sociability and ambition. The results were necessarily strongly subjective and probably failed to reflect a man's effectiveness on the job. Further distortion was introduced when salary increases or incentive payments depended on the appraisal. It was impossible for interviewer and interviewee to be entirely objective in these circumstances. A system was needed that did not rely on an assessment of nebulous character attributes, but concentrated on practical achievement. The theory of management by objectives has answered this need, but is still subject to controversy and revision. Mr John Humble, the British pioneer of management by objectives, suggests three separate appraisals instead of one:

> Performance Review.
> Potential Review.
> Salary Review.

Performance is discussed and judged against concrete targets related to overall company objectives. The more subjective potential review is kept apart and salary awards are made on actual worth to the company. A man can see that he has been assessed fairly against sensible achievable objectives and as a result feels in control of his own destiny. This approach strikes a balance between the legendary tough line and a proper appreciation of social and human values.

The seventh and eighth ingredients of our management development programme were external and internal training programmes. These are the tactics employed in the day to day process of providing the breadth and depth of knowledge and experience.

There is a great variety of methods being used. One firm will collect its staff together for a series of internal courses; another will send individual members to local courses run by technical colleges; a third encourages study in evening classes. A fourth sends men away to residential courses lasting for weeks or months and sometimes farms out men to other companies to acquire experience. Another firm may rely entirely on consultants to give training to its staff during the course of some assignment which is perhaps introducing a new technique or effecting a reorganization. Yet others may give a young man an assignment as assistant to a senior executive or use 'job rotation' or 'junior boards' as ways of enlarging experience. But perhaps the most not-

THE M.Sc. PROGRAMME

		First Year—required courses	Second Year—required courses	Elective Courses*—2nd year only
Foundations	*Quantitative methods*	Accounting I and II (M 101, M 102) Economic Analysis (M 103) Basic Mathematics (M 104) Mathematics for Optimisation (M 105) Computer Techniques (M 106) Statistics I and II (M 107, M 108) Logic and Scientific Method (M 109) 30%	Operations Research I and II (M 201, M 202)	Econometric Theory Operations Research Project Advanced Managerial Accounting
	Behavioural studies	Individual Behaviour (M 114) Organizational Behaviour (M 115) 6%	The Individual and the Organization (M 211) Personnel Management and Industrial Relations (M 212) 6%	Comparative International Organization 6%
	Environmental studies	Macroeconomics I (M 110) Industrial and Business Structure I (M 112) International Trade and Development (M 111) Corporate Legal Environment (M 113) 13%	Macroeconomics II (M 203) Industrial and Business Structure II (M 204) Managerial Dynamics (M 105) 10%	Economics of Transport
Applications	*Functional studies*		Finance I and II (M 206, M 207) Production (M 208) Marketing I and II (M 209, M 210) 17%	Portfolio Investment Advanced Production Management Information and Research for Marketing Buyer Behaviour Operational Research Application Finance and Investment
Integration	*Integrative studies*		Business Policy and Organization I and II (M 213, M 214) 6%	Any two electives
	—	49%	45%	6%

(%) denotes percentage of the total programme   * The courses listed were on offer in 1967. This list is subject to frequent amendment able achievement in management training in Britain in recent years was the foundation in 1965 of the London and Manchester Business Schools, as a result of increasing pressure from industry and commerce, assisted by Lord Robbins and Lord Franks.

Clearly only the brightest of management prospects win admittance to the Business Schools' M.Sc. two-year programmes, but the numbers increase each year as do applicants for the shorter, post-experience programmes. Further impetus was added by the doctorate programme started late in 1968. The 1968 London M.Sc. Syllabus and the extract from the prospectus shown below illustrate the urgency of modern professional attitude to business.

The aim of the programme is to equip the student with the basic knowledge required to analyse management problems and to reach and implement decisions based on that analysis. The realization of that aim requires the development of basic concepts and the acquisition of analytical tools, together with practice in their application to problems in a variety of functional fields and in pursuit of varying policy objectives. In addition a sound understanding of human relations and organization must be imparted. The concept of the manager's job that underlies the construction of the syllabus is one of complex problem-solving and decision-making. Such work requires the exercise of a wide variety of personal skills, formal analytical skills and specific skills for strategy and policy-making. The syllabus is aimed at developing these skills in the individual, and integrating them in applied work.

But London and Manchester are not the only universities offering business courses. More and more the importance of management education is being realized. In 1968 there were seventy-two universities, colleges, or business schools offering general introductory, development or specialist courses, such as the one for the Diploma in Management Studies. The demand from business is certainly being met, whether it is a technical manager requiring general management training, or a graduate wanting full-time study before taking up his first appointment.

One of the oldest established training colleges is the Administrative Staff College at Henley-on-Thames, where senior executives from public service as well as from business attend a three-month course in which the education largely derives from the exchange between men of mature experience and age, working together on the solution of a variety of problems. The contribution of Henley to management training over the last twenty years is considerable, but it will be interesting to see how it combats the competition it will inevitably meet from the new business schools.

All the activity and interest is being backed up by the Industrial Training Boards, created as a result of the Industrial Training Act, 1964. Training has been encouraged right across industry, the laggards have been goaded into action.

The Act provided for an I.T.B. for each industry or group of allied industries and within four years over twenty Boards had been established.

The Boards have three main objectives: to ensure an adequate supply of properly trained men and women at all levels; to improve the quality and efficiency of training; and to share the cost of training more evenly between firms. These objectives are achieved by means of a compulsory levy which is redistributed in the form of grants. The levy and the grant schemes vary from industry to industry, but the theory is that everybody pays and only those who train get their money back. To see fair play each Board includes directors representing the industry's Trade Unions, the employers, the Government and education.

Management training, of course, is only one of the types of training to be encouraged by the Boards. Unfortunately, to revert to a point made earlier in this chapter, it is difficult to see a return for money spent on educating managers. An increase in an operator's productivity after training can be simply calculated, but improved management performance is not so easy to define. In addition, many industries contain a large number of small companies who cannot or will not release their managers for any worthwhile period of time. This is a very real problem the Industrial Training Boards face in their formative years and Britains' prosperity at home and success in foreign markets depend in no small measure on the outcome.

Formal training, however, will never be the total answer to the development of the manager. It can give him the bricks with which to build, but the cement is of his own making. None of the theorists can yet say which of those elusive executive qualities he should have. Note the time given to behavioural studies in the London M.Sc. Programme. They can point him in the right direction, but only broad experience, self-examination and study of successful seniors will help to mould the correct approach. This sort of development takes place very much on the job.

*

If this survey is confined only to Britain's activity in the training of managers, her efforts and experiments seem exciting enough, but she cuts only a sober and matronly figure when compared with what goes on in America. Eager for experiment, unafraid to cut the losses arising from failure, generous in sharing the achievement of success, and superbly confident in man's power to mould his environment, American business has concentrated the efforts of managers, professors, sociologists and pyschologists on the problem of training, and has invested heavily in backing their findings. There has been much pioneering in many of the methods that are now used and accepted throughout the world; some of the methods indeed have not yet been fully validated and other countries are slow in endorsing them, but it is only right to acknowledge that the Americans themselves are their most rigorous critics, and are not slow in publishing their criticisms.

It is here only possible to comment on a few features of American management training practice. Certainly the most impressive and perhaps the most puzzling is the Harvard School of Business Administration. Founded in 1908, this school's main course lasts for two years, taking in each year over 700 graduates most of whom have not yet served any time within industry. The school's philosophy is a rejection of the academic teaching of a body of principles and knowledge of management, and claims instead that the only man who can teach how to manage is the student himself; he must develop his own ability to size up business problems, to ferret out the facts, to discuss it with colleagues, to make his own decisions, and then to accept the hard truth of real business life that he may never know whether his decision was in fact 'right'! For this reason the professors never profess, they never 'correct' the students, never give the school solution, their only purpose being to guide the students in the arduous process of finding out for themselves.

Harvard's main instrument for this process of self-development is the case study. Well over 20,000 of these have been compiled: each of them is a presentation of an actual situation, supported by a detailed background of facts, conditions, and history, recorded sometimes by weeks of research by an investigator.

The scale of the Harvard operation is immense (the library alone cost ten million dollars) and its prestige is such that it can take the pick of the promising young men. Its very prestige makes it difficult to judge the real validity of stressing the case study method so far, since its graduates are in any case likely to succeed in business, and will later support the Harvard method as a consequence of their own identification with it. The Harvard faculty themselves recognize the problem of validating methods of training for management, and have undertaken considerable research projects, not only to find out what improvement in a manager results from a training, but, more basically, whether there can be any method of judging improvement. The problem is not so much of finding an answer to a question, but of finding out what questions should be asked.

Until some valid, if not necessarily objective, way can be evolved of assessing methods of training, it is necessary to suspend judgement on the claims of the case study method of giving the student artificial experience, as against a more classical approach to the teaching of the theory and practice of management, and of real experience gained by spending the equivalent time in business.

The brief look at Harvard must also mention the Advanced Management Programme, a three-month course for mature senior executives who may be of president level. The role of this is similar to that of the British Henley course and the Business Schools senior management courses, though the methods used are somewhat different.

The bright light of Harvard tends to eclipse the smaller, but now equally successful schools at the Massachusetts Institute of Technology, Carnegie and Stanford, to mention just three. The objectives of all the schools are naturally similar, it is the curricula that differ. No other school puts as much emphasis on the case method as Harvard, although cases are used in association with more traditional media. Carnegie is especially strong in communicating the quantitative techniques of scientific management. M.I.T.'s Alfred P. Sloan School of Management boasts excellent departments in the social sciences and economics. Stanford has an equally high general reputation.

In fact most American universities offer a course in Business Administration. This is a normal step for a young man planning a business career and contrasts with many of his counterparts in Britain who are studying arts subjects, intended to educate them generally, or technical subjects, such as engineering, intended to qualify them in the practice of a profession.

*

The young aspirant to a career as a manager, wondering how he can best equip himself by study and experience for this most arduous yet most rewarding of responsibilities, may well be perplexed at the variety of paths from which he must make a choice. Business school postgraduate course, technical apprenticeship, evening classes, sandwich course? – the decision is important as he will be committing much of his time and energy to it – and these are the main resources out of which he must build his career. For his guidance, the British Institute of Management publishes a manual on training courses, If the sheer numbers confuse the young enquirer he may find help at the B.I.M. Management Education Information Unit.

It may be some comfort to him to know that the seasoned personnel director is no less perplexed when confronted with the problem of how best to ensure for his organization a planned succession of men with the right character, experience, and training to fill each management position as it falls vacant. Job rotation, role playing, business games, external courses, Harvard, the local 'tech', group dynamics – all these make strong claims for his backing, but can they all be right?

It is a truism that whereas in the physical sciences one can usually find an exact, objective, usually quantitative answer to any problem, in the human sciences one must be reconciled to finding answers of a subjective, statistical nature; the difficulty of finding answers is multiplied by the impossibility of eliminating all the variables. They may be right on the average, but it is a matter of probability whether they fit the individual case.

One must therefore still rely on the accumulated experience of centuries, trying to establish basic principles which have stood the test of time and have also stood up to the searching criticism of the last decade. This criticism has thrown over many false idols, but has been ready to confirm what it has found to be of value. Regarded in this light, there are three pillars on which any management education should be firmly based – Example, Experience, and Knowledge.

Example is perhaps the most potent means of learning: the opportunity to observe, in action, somebody one can admire and respect. Earlier in this book the responsibility of top management to secure, all the way down the line, an understanding of the need to set an example and to communicate the business objectives has been stressed. Any executive with younger, aspiring men under him must be made aware, if such awareness is not instinct within him, of his duty to the business to set an example to those he is concerned with developing.

The second essential, which also bears greatly on the question of developing subordinates, is Experience. Men learn to know themselves, as well as their jobs, by trying out in practice what they have learned by precept or ideas they have conceived themselves; by solving the problems that arise, by correcting the mistakes they make and taking the blame for mistakes they can't correct, they acquire the confidence of their fellows and their own confidence in themselves, necessary still to further development.

It is important, however, that such experience should be guided by a senior man, who can choose the right experience his junior should undergo and should guide him with advice and help lest he wastes too much energy and enthusiasm and becomes frustrated. Every senior manager must therefore recognize his responsibility for giving this guidance, and should not shirk it under the slogan 'Throw 'em in – the bad ones will sink, and the good ones swim'. There are many examples in business life of the men who might have been good managers if only they were given the right encouragement at the crucial stages in their careers. An early chapter in this book called them 'managers-who-might-have-been' and there are too many of them around.

One of the contributions made by the American 'executive development schemes' is their emphasis on the guidance or 'counselling' by the superior of his subordinate. Granted that the American approach may sometimes over-emphasize the methodology of the 'appraisal' and the 'appraisal interview', it is entirely right in its insistence that the superior should face up to his responsibility for advice, praise or blame and discuss the subordinate's performance.

It is also necessary that the experience should be extended and varied according to an individual plan. Many a man with 'ten years' experience' has really only one year's experience repeated ten times over. Much of the process of learning management is the experience of a new job, a new department, and new colleagues, and this can be provided by arranging suitable cross postings or planning ladders of promotion. Even in minor ways, attendance at courses or visits to exhibitions or other plants enlarge experience. And this is an appropriate point to mention the 'sabbatical year'. Too few businesses, as their managers approach the pinnacle of top executive responsibility, are courageous or far-seeing enough to give a year – or even six months – off, on full salary, with no strings attached. It is the 'no strings' aspect that is vital. Maybe a manager has always longed to write a book, or to start learning the flute, or to travel to Benares, or to lose weight. No matter how far away from the business objectives the pursuits of those precious months may be, it must be of priceless value for a man or woman once or twice at least in a business career to be able to get right outside and take stock not just of himself or herself but of life. The traditional annual holiday is just not enough: only a long break with uncommitted time on one's hands can achieve the object.

Example and experience give training in the 'How' of management: of the 'What' of management much can be learnt in the course of normal working at the various jobs a man holds. With the increasing technical complexity, size, and control requirements, however, there is accumulating a body of social, economic, and managerial practice which the competent manager must acquire. He need not be an expert in many of these branches, but he must understand what the experts are talking about, he must know what the experts can do and what they cannot do: he must in fact be able to manage them.

For much of this knowledge the young manager must be responsible himself. On his own initiative he must read widely, he must be ready, indeed eager, to talk to any experts he can buttonhole, he must keep abreast of the technical press, and he must attend institution meetings and conferences. But for other parts of his knowledge he has the right to expect that his firm shall make provision.

A final chapter will try to sum up the main challenges that the manager of tomorrow, managing in the technological age that lies ahead when automation in every form of business activity will be accepted technique, will have to face. His training will be of immense importance, and too few people are thinking ahead about this problem today.

10

Successful Management

SUCCESS is a fugitive concept but readers of the following stories will discern, it is hoped, many of the characteristics of good management which this book has been discussing in earlier chapters. In arranging them the writer has been concerned to give examples of companies whose success can be fairly attributed to different sorts of business emphasis. Thus Rowntree* might be described as being essentially marketing-oriented; Triplex, production-oriented; Tilling, a classic example of the industrial holding company concerned with use of finance; Metals Research Ltd, a remarkable growth story oriented to technology or, more simply, research and development. But the writer wishes to make it clear that the word 'oriented' does not mean that the successes can be solely attributed to a particular orientation; it is merely to underline possibly the most dominating 'drive' in the company's progression. Let the stories, however, speak for themselves.

ROWNTREE MACKINTOSH LTD

'Back kitchen methods' is a phrase used at Rowntrees today to describe the production process of any confectionery that does not lend itself to a modern mass production line. How often does the user of this disparaging term stop to recall that it was in a back kitchen in 1725 that the Rowntree business started life? Then Mrs Tuke's mouth-watering recipes were known only to the children of York; today the

*This piece about Rowntrees was written just prior to their merger with John Mackintosh & Sons Ltd.

company is the second largest producer of chocolate and confectionery in the United Kingdom, and is the centre of an international group of companies which employs well over 20,000 people throughout the world.

For the first 150 years the Quaker Tukes and the Rowntrees, who took over in 1862, built a reputation for good drinking chocolate and cocoa. In 1879 quite fortuitously a Frenchman arrived in York to persuade Henry and Joseph Rowntree to give him facilities to start making pastilles and gums. Thus were laid the foundations of a business new to this country which still makes a major contribution to the company's turnover. A significant pointer to the future marketing philosophy was that, even at this early stage, the improved profitability was used to obtain better machinery to produce better products more efficiently.

Expansion continued under a family as concerned with the country's social problems as with running a business. But in 1930 Rowntree's attitude to its products and its markets changed. George Harris, after several years' experience of selling in the home market and in the United States, was appointed Marketing Manager and later Marketing Director. He inherited a price list of incredible complexity. Over 100 different lines and 250 different packs were being produced in small lots at considerable cost to the company.

Harris looked at his market in those depressed days of the early thirties and established a marketing strategy which was still relevant after the tremendous disruptions of the war and rationing. Thus, the company was able to pick up the marketing threads where they had been left in 1939. The policies he evolved remain the heart of the company's philosophy today and are undoubtedly the reason for Rowntree's success in a highly competitive situation. He saw that the name Rowntree was associated in the consumer's mind with fruit gums and pastilles, table jellies, and cocoa. New products must create their own fresh image. He saw that the consumer wanted something good to eat at a reasonable price. If the product was priced above the market it would never obtain high volume sales. He foresaw a streamlined factory producing perhaps only twenty high volume lines, achieving not only the right selling price but also the right profit through the economies of scale. He saw that it would be necessary to sell products at a loss, perhaps for two or three years, until aggressive selling and mass advertising created the right volume of sales.

George Harris gathered round him a team of scientists, finance men, advertising and market research people and it must have been an interesting board meeting that day in 1933 when he put forward their plan to market their first new product, Black Magic. It probably seemed commercial suicide to sell a chocolate assortment, normally costing 4s. in a frilly box, for 2s. 10d in a simple black and white carton. But they had discovered the centres most acceptable to the consumer, they had developed a quality product at the right price, and the romantic aura in which they surrounded it carried Black Magic to the leadership of its market. Over thirty years later it is still there.

Harris was careful never to make a direct attack on a competitive product. Working closely with his team he researched the market to find gaps and make, as it were, a flanking attack. Before the war came, with its constraints on raw material supplies, Kit Kat, Aero, Dairy Box and Smarties were added to Black Magic and all well and truly launched. Excepting Dairy Box, each one had its unique selling point.

During the war sugar rationing and lack of essential raw materials forced some companies to lower their standards. Rowntree, however, refused to allow their branded products to move on to this slippery slope. Black Magic, for instance, was taken out of production so as not to mar its unique brand image and consequently endanger its safe return at a later date. It was another case of planning ahead and taking a long term view. The years of deprivation did not deter new product developments but seriously interfered with their realization and in fact Polo Mints alone reached the market.

George Harris retired in 1952, but his basic marketing philosophy lives on at Rowntrees. After Eight was launched in 1962, perhaps one of the greatest post-war marketing successes in any field. Jellytots, Walnut Whips and Matchmakers have followed, and although the company has fewer than twenty standard lines, ten of them are market leaders.

In order to understand Rowntree's strategy for the 1970s, it is important to look in some detail at its traditional market in the United Kingdom. In 1958 the people of Great Britain consumed more chocolate and sugar confectionery in total than in 1967. Sales were deflated by Purchase Tax in 1962 and are only gradually climbing back to the 600,000 tons a year level and even this can be partially accounted for by the natural population increase. It should be added, however, that we already consume more chocolate and sugar confectionery per head than any other nation. Only the Swiss eat more chocolate per head. It would seem that an intake of about 8oz. of confectionery per head per week is a natural barrier through which it may be impossible to break. There are so many other ways in which sugar enters the daily diet that 8oz. may be the physiological limit.

There is also a limit to what the consumer will pay. The imposition of Purchase Tax and the general increase in costs has made it difficult to hold the unit prices which are so important to this industry. On the other hand, it could be said that the abandonment of retail price maintenance and the pressure of government agencies has restricted the industry's freedom in the area of prices. Which is the right course of action – to reduce quantity or quality or to increase price? This is assuming, of course, that it is impossible to reduce internal costs.

Costs have perhaps been the greatest single factor in

shaping the industry. Volume sales have permitted investment in high capacity, special purpose production machinery, which in turn has enabled the larger companies to keep
quality high and price relatively low. The smaller companies
operating typically in a limited segment of the market are
unable to take advantage of the economies of scale. Not for
them are the trackless forests of the national market and
too often is the home farm plundered by the marauding
giants. The 1960s have seen membership of the Cocoa,
Chocolate and Confectionery Alliance decline from about
500 to 225 companies. There is no doubt that this trend will
continue to the benefit, in particular, of the four largest
companies, Cadbury-Fry, Rowntree, Mars and Mackintosh.
The big four, of which Cadbury-Fry is very much the biggest,
took well over half the market in 1967. Since the total
market is almost static the fight for growth is to the death
and only the fittest survive.

The industry serves 250,000 outlets. It faces all the usual
problems of the fast moving consumer goods business – how
far down the scale should direct calling be maintained? At
what level should the multiples be approached, and what
propositions should be put to them? What attitude should
be taken with wholesalers and cash and carry warehouses?
What sort of distribution? What sort of packing? and so
on. . . . And yet when these questions are answered only
a small part of the marketing mix has been settled.

Against this background, Rowntree's plans for growth and
profitability are based on five fundamental policies:

(a) Resources are concentrated on a limited range of high
     volume branded goods.
(b) Each established product is treated as a separate, self-
     funding business.
(c) Decisions are taken with an eye on continuity and the
     long term future.

(d) Not only is every opportunity taken to expand through new or existing products on the home market, but also a continuing effort is made to establish proven products in markets overseas.

(e) The company will diversify into operations complementary to its own.

In 1966 the company split into five operating divisions, namely U.K. Confectionery, U.K. Grocery, Overseas and Export, Europe, and Supply and Transport. Each division has a board of executives representing the major functions – it is worth noting that three out of the eleven members of the U.K. Confectionery division board are marketeers. All the divisional chairmen and some other members of the divisional boards sit on the Group Board which consists wholly of full-time executive directors. These are the teams of men who carry forward the policies formulated by George Harris over thirty years ago. Rowntree has a place in history; it is a household name. But meanwhile, several million pounds' worth of unique machinery for putting the hole in the mint or the sugar on the Smarties has to be kept turning twenty-four hours a day. Sales cannot be allowed to flag.

The first line of attack is obviously the sales force, but responsibility for staying one jump ahead, not only of the competitor but also of market trends, lies with the brand managers and their advertising agents. It has always been the policy to work closely with the agencies as if they were another division of the company. The products are shared round three different agencies, so that there is a constant flow of fresh ideas. The brief is to squeeze out every last ounce of profitable growth, and, as each brand has to be self supporting, the motivation is strong. It is marketing in the broadest sense – everything from a tireless pursuit of the minutiae of market research to the consumer benefits derived from the constant improvements in mass production techniques – that sustains growth and continuity.

Rowntree advertising has given birth to several classic slogans. 'Have a break, have a Kit Kat' and 'Don't forget the Fruit Gums' have been running for over ten years; 'Polo – The Mint with the Hole' for over twenty years. There have been many others, but perhaps even more fascinating has been the way Rowntrees have created an upper class, aristocratic image for products, particularly After Eight and Black Magic, which sell on the mass market. It is a curious mental somersault from white tie and tails at the opera or *après diner* at the Savoy to 'jam butties' in front of the telly.

The brand manager uses all the modern tools of market research to monitor the quality and stability of his brand. Consumers' purchases and attitudes are watched through the Nielsen and many other research services so that brand weaknesses or strengths are detected before they have a marked effect on sales. Every small detail in the marketing mix must be validated. And yet despite the sophistication there is the ever present concern, as in all consumer goods industries, to improve the techniques for measuring the exact effectiveness of advertising.

The search for new chocolate or sugar confectionery products goes on at York and within the advertising agencies. But there is a limit to the variations possible on a theme and the future will see a greater contribution to growth from overseas markets and from diversification. Diversification already includes biscuits, nuts, pickles and warehousing and transport, all of which utilize existing resources and experience. Abroad, the company has had for many years and is still developing local manufacturing and marketing units in Canada, Australia and South Africa. Rowntree made a further major move, when they went into the European market of 200 million people, by setting up a manufacturing and marketing base in Hamburg in 1965. In all these countries, the long term policy is to build a lasting business in Rowntree staple lines. A firmly based marketing operation requires considerable expenditure on development costs and where necessary losses are accepted in the short term, but as always Rowntree have their sights on the next decade.

Rowntree's success on the marketing front is obvious to the world. Beneath it, however, lies a strong foundation of sophisticated financial control, high ability in the technical field, considerable achievement on the productivity front and, last but by no means least, a strong community spirit based on the social and industrial relations policies of the founder of the business and his successors.

TRIPLEX SAFETY GLASS CO. LTD

Triplex Safety Glass Co. Ltd is a creature of the motor age. It came into being before the first war, manufacturing laminated glass on a modest scale under a licence from the French inventors. In those days safety glass was an optional novelty and motorists and their passengers continued to be killed and mutilated by flying plate glass when their cars became involved in accidents. By the time Parliament imposed the legal obligation that all windscreens should be safety glass (in 1937) nearly all vehicles already had toughened or laminated windscreens, and when it finally became compulsory to use safety glass for all vehicle windows in the early fifties, the need for compulsion was similarly no longer pressing.

Now, more than half a century since its inception, Triplex Safety Glass Company supplies virtually all the British Motor Industry's requirements of safety glass. Triplex is the only safety glass manufacturer of any size in the country; its market is assured, its output will continue to grow in step with the growth of its customers; and its sales to the motor industry which currently amount to over £16½m. a year are expected to rise to well over £20m. a year in the coming decade.

Triplex is a subsidiary of its supplier of raw material, the giant glass manufacturer, Pilkington Brothers Ltd. Though the Pilkington holding is increasing, it still only stands at around 60 per cent of the total Triplex equity and is not increasing by more than $1\frac{1}{2}$–2 per cent each year. Pilkington, unlike its counterparts in other vehicle producing countries, did not enter the safety glass field from the start in direct competition with the independent companies. Instead, realizing the potential of the motor market for glass, it adopted the policy of cooperation with encouragement from the strongest safety glass manufacturer – Triplex. Ever since the early 1920s there have been intimate links between the companies, but the management of Triplex has remained self-sufficient. There has always existed a hidden threat that Pilkington could put Triplex out of business if the management of Triplex ever took so independent a line as to jeopardize Pilkington interests; but the long-term interests of the two companies have always been so closely allied that no serious differences of opinion have ever arisen. It is true that Triplex is gradually being bought up by Pilkington, and no doubt will one day become a wholly owned subsidiary. It is Pilkington's declared intention, however, that the management – that is the day-to-day control of Triplex – should not become integrated with that of Pilkington.

Triplex is primarily orientated towards production. In the early days of the 1920s sales representatives were sent round to motor racing meetings to sell safety glass to chauffeurs, and the company advertised extensively in order to create demand for its products. Nowadays, as we have seen, the demand exists automatically for practically all Triplex products other than minor optional lines like electrically heated rear windows; and the company's main effort must, therefore, be not to stimulate further demand, for further demand is self-generating, but to satisfy existing demand in the most efficient and economical manner possible. It must also ensure that sufficient capacity is available in time to meet the ever higher peaks which occur with only moderate predictability in the production cycle of the British motor industry.

Triplex, like its parent, is a monopoly – it faces no competition in the United Kingdom as a supplier of glass to the large motor manufacturers. It has always dominated the industry, but has not always been a monopoly. On three occasions the position of the company has been seriously threatened, but on each the final outcome has been that the serious competitor has either merged with Triplex or been bought out by it and closed down. On none of these three occasions has it been necessary for Triplex to lower its prices to unremunerative levels in order to embarrass its smaller and more narrowly based rivals. The reason for this is simple. Apart from any merit on the side of production and technical management, the Company has been forced to offer the right prices by the very nature of its market; as the largest operator in the field, it has therefore been obliged to be the most efficient, producing the best product at the lowest overall cost to its customers. These customers decrease in number and increase in size from year to year. Most of them have affiliations with motor manufacturers abroad – in Europe and the United States, and are thus in a position to form an accurate notion of how much their components should cost. They are also quite large enough and technically quite competent enough to set up their own safety glass plants in the United Kingdom or Europe, following the successful examples of Chrysler and Ford in America. If such a situation ever arose, and Pilkington and the motor manufacturers were unable to come to an arrangement, either together or separately to make Triplex once more internationally competitive, Pilkington could never afford to protect its subsidiary by specially favourable terms of supply.

The technological content of safety glass is low, and safety glass production is no longer subject to any generic patents for the time being. Triplex has never been a great innovator, and the major developments in safety glass have always come from abroad. Laminated glass produced by the old cellulose method which led to the glass turning yellow with age was originally invented by a French chemist, and the old Triplex Safety Class Company was formed to exploit his patents. Toughened glass, which in these days accounts for more than 90 per cent of safety glass used on British cars, was similarly a French invention, sublicensed in the early nineteen thirties by Pilkington to Triplex. After the second war in 1945, an improved method of producing laminated glass was introduced under licence from America, and since then technological advance in the safety glass industry has confined itself to refining the properties and qualities of existing types, and to improving and developing the machines that produce them.

Triplex has not suffered as a result of its lack of innovation, being in an industry in which the cost of royalties would certainly have been less than the cost of setting up a research organization of sufficient size to stimulate an innovatory attitude. Most of the counterparts of Triplex in other countries are fully integrated with their glass manufacturing parent companies, and their technical development falls into the overall technical programmes of their parent. Until Triplex became a subsidiary of Pilkington, it was too small to engage in a full-time research programme on anything like the scale of its competitors. Since Pilkington gained control, however, it has had full access to Pilkington's extensive laboratories, and has extended its own engineering and development division.

In the course of the last fifteen years, Triplex has had to centralize its management functions. Before that, the company consisted of three separate factories, one in Lancashire which was jointly owned with Pilkington, one in Birmingham, and one in London. Each works was controlled by a Works Director who was responsible to the Board for the profits his factory made; beyond that, there was little coordination and paperwork, accounting methods, production technique and conditions of employment tended to be different at each works. The change came about gradually, prompted chiefly by the switch from flat to curved windscreens and rear windows. The production of curved glass could not be transferred freely between the factories, and a central form of production control became necessary. This was balanced by a central sales organization and a new policy of considering company profitability as a whole at the expense of the profitability of individual works.

As the company has grown, it has become more complicated – not because what it is doing has changed in any fundamental respect, but because increased size breeds more intricate organization and administration. Consequently a determined effort has been made to rationalize the old organization in such a way as to maintain maximum flexibility.

Triplex has grown on the sound basis of a reliable expanding market from being a small speculative business through being a collection of medium sized businesses into being the large and well-established firm it is now. Provided it continues to concentrate its corporate consciousness on the virtues of foresight and economy, its foreseeable future is sunny.

THE TILLING GROUP

There can be no doubt that the Tilling Group is one of the most successful companies of its type in this country, judged by a comparatively long record of steady progress in profits and return on shareholders' funds. This is a good example of how money can be made to work by a small but good management, without a massive central organization or an excessive number of technical experts. There are, of course, other successful industrial holding companies, some with more dynamic recent growth, but they are mostly much smaller than Tillings and they still have to prove themselves over the long haul. There have also been some spectacular failures, and for this reason the image in financial circles of the industrial holding company is not always favourable. It is said that control from the centre in such companies tends be too loose, and that there is insufficient knowledge there of what is going on in the companies. However, talking to Mr Kenneth Chapman, the managing director of Tillings, who is a lawyer, and to Mr Stanley Harding, the financial director, in their headquarters at Crewe House in Curzon Street, it was not difficult to see why this group has been successful. They are fully aware of the problems and are constantly striving to improve their techniques: they have time to think and plan as good managers should do, without being swamped by day-to-day matters.

Tilling funds were derived originally from the nationalization of Thomas Tilling's transport interest and in 1949 they retained £5m. in cash out of the £25m. which they received from the Government, returning £20m. to the shareholders. Since then, in twenty years, under chairman Lionel Fraser followed by Sir Geoffrey Eley, group sales have risen to £160m. and profits to more than £9m. There are some 150 companies, of which 30 are large direct subsidiaries, and the group is among the first hundred of British companies. It is interesting and an education to look at their annual accounts which give the shareholders a detailed report of the directors' stewardship and show, for instance, that profits have more than trebled over the past ten years as have the dividends, and that the return on equity capital and reserves is well above 20 per cent. It would be more realistic today to regard Tillings as a 'blue chip' rather than as a member of the somewhat mixed community of industrial holding companies or conglomerates.

Growth has been by the acquisition of new companies and by the development of existing companies, but today expansion is naturally more through the existing companies. As a generality some 75 per cent of all new money has been pumped into these whilst 25 per cent has gone into acquisitions. The type of company which finds Tillings attractive is the private company with problems of death duties, close company taxation, management succession, or where the shares are in trust but the eggs still all in one basket. This type of situation can be very worrying for a man who has built up, by hard work and in the face of considerable risks, a business which may be worth well above £1m. He is happy to join forces with Tillings since, whilst retaining a considerable measure of autonomy and continuing to run his company in his own name, he can get the financial backing and the protection and commercial assistance of a very powerful group. Such a private company, if successful, could of course get financial backing from banking sources or it could go public; but in the former case it would be unlikely to get the management support which it gets from Tillings, and in the latter it would have to deal with a mass of faceless shareholders which can be intimidating if things are not going well.

A significant development has taken place quite recently – namely the approach to Tillings by a number of public companies which for one reason or another, often the fear of an unwelcome takeover by a competitor, wish to join the Group. At the same time Tillings, whilst not ignoring the possibilities which will always exist among private companies, are themselves raising their sights and are on the look-out for public companies whose activities fit in with their own long-term objectives. All this could lead to a pattern of much larger acquisitions by Tillings in the future, as already evidenced by activity in 1969 when Tillings have acquired several other public companies in exchange for their own shares.

Tillings is probably the largest group of its type in Europe, but there are others in the U.S.A. which are bigger, such as Litton Industries. Some people think that Tillings is an investment trust with a purely financial interest in the companies, shuffling the pack as it thinks fit, picking up a company here and dropping one there, but this is far from being the case. They are deeply involved in the fortunes of their companies and work closely with the men who run them.

For the purpose of this chapter it is unnecessary to touch upon aspects of Tillings which are common to any well-run business, but it may be of interest to consider the special problems peculiar to such a group. A criticism often levelled is that, by having a spread of business over several industries, what is gained on the swings can be lost on the roundabouts, and that it is better for a company to be more deeply committed in one industry. This may be true if such a group is badly managed, but if it is well managed then it has room to manoeuvre and can increase its stake in the industries which offer the greatest potential for growth. Tillings at present are mainly involved in building materials and merchanting, engineering, furniture, glassware, insurance, publishing, textiles, vehicle distribution, and electrical wholesaling, and it is their intention to build upon these industries about which they know a great deal. Many of the companies have household names – for instance Pretty Polly stockings, Heinemann Books, Pyrex glassware and Cornhill Insurance. As many as seven of the companies are annually earning more than £500,000 each, and three earn more than £1m. each. This gives Tillings a firm base on which to build and plan their growth; it is a weakness of some of the newer and smaller industrial holding groups that a serious set-back in any one part of the business can rock the whole edifice.

One of the fascinating things about Tillings is that a number of the companies are still run by the original owners, and with the same enthusiasm as always despite the fact that they may now hold none or only a small percentage of the equity. This is because they have been allowed to retain their individuality and the staff still look to them as the boss – Tillings are in the background but always there in case of need. This is the way to handle a man who has shown himself capable of building up a valuable business by his own sweat. It would be out of the question to attempt to browbeat him or to mould him to a rigid pattern. This, however, poses the biggest problem in running such a group – how to achieve and retain satisfactory control over a giant empire, whilst allowing the component parts freedom to continue operating in a substantially unchanged manner. Many companies are able to grow to a certain point despite weaknesses in management, in control, or in financial structure; Tillings can put these matters right and enable the company to move into a bigger league. As regards money it can also inject the benefit of gearing by borrowing money centrally on favourable terms, and this can transform a satisfactory return on total funds into a very attractive return on the shareholders' funds.

There is nothing static about Tillings. The top group of men at the centre have all had wide commercial or professional experience before they joined the group and each new man who joins asks the sort of questions about the group's policy which would be asked by an outside management consultant, and there is the minimum of resistance to new suggestions. The total personnel numbers in the group exceed 25,000 but there is only a handful, mostly of experts, at the centre which means that the burden of paperwork between the centre and the operating companies is kept down to the minimum. The link man between the centre and the operating companies is a Tilling executive, who is the chairman of five or six direct subsidiaries, with a small team of assistants. He is the man who encourages his companies to expand profitably, who participates in planning and policy decisions without getting involved in the day to day affairs of the company, and who is in essence the company's friend and adviser. If fire fighting is called for when things go wrong in a company, as they must inevitably do from time to time, then this man is able to call upon the group's financial director and others for assistance. Speedy decisions are easy to achieve in such an atmosphere, and there are a number of services available at the centre in such fields as law, taxation, pensions, property, computers, etc. It would be all too easy when acquiring a profitable private company to impose upon it excessively high standards and a burden of overheads which would soon turn profits into losses. Tillings are well aware of this danger and they keep their head office small with this in mind.

The fact that the companies are independent operating units facilitates the methods of control which become increasingly important as the group grows in size. These are based mainly upon three year forecasts, monthly reporting against targets, and a realistic control on capital expenditure. The annual forecasts are revised at the half year, and the figures are discussed each month at an executive committee meeting and at the board meeting when the Tilling men representing the companies have to justify to their colleagues the performance of their companies. The first principle of good control is readily apparent – that individuals are held accountable for performance. The essence of control in Tillings is that once the checks have been built into the system then there is not a constant chivvying of the operators. Those at the top will, as it were, pull the pieces of wool on the pullover: if the strands hold firm then the system is sound, but if they show signs of giving way then the whole thing could come to pieces and remedial action is taken without delay.

On the acquisition front it is, of course, easy enough to buy profits, but Tillings make sure that the profits they buy are adequate in relation to the funds which will need to be employed. They value a company on its ability to earn profits, but they also look for adequate asset backing. Up to now the acquisitions have all been on the basis of a willing seller and a willing buyer, but with Tillings' recent more aggressive policy this may not always be the case in future. It was interesting to note that Tillings do all their own investigations and this gives them an insight from the very start into a company's activities and a close knowledge of the men running it. They say that reports on investigations by third parties tend to concentrate too much upon the bare bones and figures of a company, giving insufficient indication of the quality of the personalities involved or of the market and the competition. Tillings' acquisition policy is to buy big into a new industry, but they put no minimum limit upon size if they are building upon existing companies. They also like to leave the vendor with a stake in his business as an incentive.

Although they have a remarkably good record of successful acquisition they are well aware of the danger of overconfidence, and by distinguishing clearly between taking a chance and taking a risk they avoid ending up with a 'dog's breakfast' of problem companies on their plate. With a rather large share of their business in the United Kingdom they acknowledge the need to expand more quickly overseas, but so far they have found this easier to do through their existing companies than by direct acquisition which tends to be more difficult abroad than in the United Kingdom.

Tillings are playing an important part in the economy of

the country – by developing private companies to a size which would entitle them to rank as quite large public companies. What is also of importance for the country is that Tilling companies offer exceptional opportunities for young men, who tend to get responsibility at an earlier age than they might do elsewhere. They are well aware of the importance of size in reducing unit costs and increasing buying power, but they are proving that a company does not have to be monolithic to succeed. Indeed, except in certain very capital intensive industries, size may encourage rigidity and complacency. This is borne out by statistics which show that the return on capital employed by medium sized companies, with sales of up to £10m. and profits of up to £1m., is usually superior to that of much bigger companies. This is the strength of Tillings – a group of well-chosen and well-run medium sized companies in which the top man is still known and respected by the majority of his employees. Tillings is not just a story of financial success – it is a lesson in human relations, rapid communications and flexibility.

METALS RESEARCH LTD

Metals Research Ltd is a young but extremely successful company working from a modern factory near Cambridge. It is at present operating in the sophisticated, fast developing fields of materials technology and image analysis, which latter technique is explained below. To survive at all in these fields of operation a company must not only be generally well managed and sensitive to its markets, but it must also be totally geared to the generation and development of new products. This kind of development is not possible without the deployment of brains of exceptional ability. Such brains are wasted unless pointed in the right direction.

Initially, Metals Research's brains were those of the

founder, Dr Michael Cole. From the age of sixteen he had been developing an ambition to build up a large organization for turning inventions into profitable hardware. At that age he was thinking in terms of mechanical and electronic devices mainly connected with cars, boats and household appliances. However, despite an obvious interest in engineering, having specialized in science at Eton, he went on to read Natural Sciences at Cambridge.

He won his degree but had no money to realize his ambition and therefore decided to remain temporarily in academic life. He stayed at Cambridge and acquired a Ph.D. in metallurgy, took a research fellowship in Chicago for a year and returned to Cambridge for two more years of metallurgical research.

During these last two years Michael Cole's ideas on the type of business he wanted to establish began to emerge. He saw that the safest way to build it up was to make some highly specialized product that required great skill and knowledge in relation to the value of its market but which would be highly sought after by enough people to make it pay. A product of this sort would be immune from competition from small concerns because of its technical content and from large firms because of its small market. When the business grew on the profits from the first product, a new product with a larger market would be introduced and so on. The only question was – what should the first product be?

He got the idea quite by chance whilst dining in a pub near Cambridge with four eminent academics from different English universities. One of them complained bitterly that he had been trying to do a very simple experiment for six months but had been held up because he had failed to grow the single crystal of brass which the experiment demanded: once he had this crystal the experiment could be completed in a matter of hours. The other dons each said they had met similar difficulties in the past and Cole suddenly recalled the desperation of a German scientist who had worked next door to him in Chicago. For months this researcher had been unable to produce a single crystal of nickel on which hinged a brief but exciting experiment.

He realized that the experience of the four diners was a reflection of the difficulties encountered by scientists the world over. There was no method of producing single crystals satisfactorily or economically for the average laboratory. He thought that a central organization, especially set up to make crystals, could, after it had produced the equipment and established the recipes, satisfy this need. Immediately deciding that this was the product he was looking for he invited one of his fellow diners – Dr T. P. Hoar, a lecturer in Metallurgy at Cambridge, and his ex-Ph.D. Supervisor – to be a director in the proposed company. The invitation was accepted on the understanding that his role would be mainly advisory.

The initial capital was subscribed by a small group of friends, many of them Cambridge dons, and Metals Research Ltd was incorporated in Cambridge in November, 1957.

There was indeed a demand for single crystals but their manufacture proved harder than expected. Michael Cole soon found which ones he could make and started to get research contracts from government and industry to discover ways of making those he could not. As increased technology in industry created demands for new materials, the sponsored research activity grew larger than crystal production and the company were researching into things other than crystals: the reputation of Metals Research as specialists spread and by 1959 research contracts from American and Australian government departments had been received.

The special machines developed for cutting and shaping the crystals and the special furnaces for growing them turned out to have a substantial market. This equipment was promoted and demand built up so rapidly that this activity soon became larger than crystals and sponsored research.

In five years the company had grown from three to forty-five people and it was obvious that still more rapid growth lay ahead. Its products were being sold in about twenty countries and the operation was beginning to become profitable and more complex. The important thing was to maintain control over all the functions of the business to ensure a smooth passage between the Scylla of finance and the Charybdis of 'boffinry'. Gradually a management team was being constructed. Michael Cole's brother David, an arts graduate, joined the company to build up the commercial side and lay the foundations for an international marketing organization which would clearly soon be needed.

Metals Research was never short of its own ideas for new products, but as it became known as an enterprising manufacturer of sophisticated scientific materials and equipment, scientists started to come to Cambridge with their inventions. Ideas for new scientific products started flowing in from sources in government, university and industry. Most of them, though promising, needed too much capital or special marketing facilities, and had to be rejected. One, however, turned out to be very important, although it was not adopted directly. A government scientist who owned a Metals Research machine came to Cambridge to discuss it. During the visit, he enquired whether the Coles would be interested in manufacturing a device he had built for scanning microscope photographs of metals for automatic measurement of their grain size. They were interested and circularized a hundred likely buyers to discover whether they would purchase such a device if it were offered at £500. The response was discouraging but all the steel companies they approached said that if an alternative device were offered they would buy several even if they cost thousands of pounds. The suggestion was that the device should look directly at the metal down the microscope without needing an intermediate photographic step. It should not only count the grains but also assess the amount of non-metallic debris in the steel. Further market research encouraged the Coles to drop the original idea and develop an instrument as suggested.

Up to this point, Michael Cole had personally organized the development of most of the company's products, but in December, 1963, Colin Fisher, who had just finished his Ph.D. research in Plasma Physics, joined the company to set up a formal development department. His first task was to develop this new instrument with all speed. In fact, Fisher had already proved his worth to Metals Research by designing an extremely successful spark erosion machine during a summer vacation job. The company wisely kept in close contact with him throughout his academic career and three years after he joined he became Technical Director.

The instrument was duly developed in record time and proved an immediate success. The Quantimet Image Analysing Computer, as it was called, has been bought by most of the major steel companies in the main steel producing countries and is well on its way to becoming a world standard for control of non-metallic inclusions in steel. In 1968 it was the first and only Image Analysing Computer on the market and earned the company the Queen's Award to Industry for technological innovation. But the company is far from resting on its laurels. The forty-strong development team are not wasting the long lead they have established over competitors right across their product range. Quantimet particularly, with its ability to peer down a microscope, replacing fallible operators for such tasks as counting and sizing particles, has a long future ahead. Opportunities are being prized open for it in mineralogy, medicine, air pollution, pharmaceutics and food technology. A thoroughly professional marketing organization ensures that the company's resources are applied to its products and markets in the most effective way. Decisions are taken by management after consideration of the facts, whereas, although Metals Research has never been a 'seat of the pants' operation, in the early days people, money and time were never available to provide information in depth.

The company's products have a strong appeal to Western Europe, North America and the more highly industrialized Iron Curtain countries. It is in these areas that the main export sales effort is concentrated. The policy initially was to set up exclusive distributorships except behind the Iron Curtain where selling was direct. In 1967 a Metals Research selling company was established in France and the intention, particularly in America and Germany, is to extend this approach.

Turnover in 1968 reached £1m. and £2m. is the pro-ected target for 1970. A considerable proportion of the 1970 figure will certainly come from newly developed products. This rapid expansion will involve doubling the number of employees within two years to five hundred. It will also aim at providing additional factory space, either by extension or acquisition.

The first ten years of Metals Research's life saw it rise to compete successfully and profitably in its own field with the best and biggest in the world. A group of gifted and keen amateurs has become an efficient professional organization. The driving enthusiasm, which contributed so much to its success is still there: innovation flourishes in a stimulating, even informal atmosphere. The management team now has a breadth and depth which Dr Michael Cole is convinced is the most important single contributory factor to the next ten years' success.

CAMBRIDGE CONSULTANTS LTD

As a postscript to a chapter on successful management, the story of Cambridge Consultants has been added as being uniquely interesting for its unusual emphasis on brains rather than brawn. While in America it is by no means unusual to find companies whose sole activity is providing expertise in research and development, in England such companies are a rarity. Moreover, Cambridge Consultants is one of the very few groups in the world which concentrates on sponsored development as opposed to sponsored research. A research project generally calls for an unspecified improvement in something or for the expenditure of money in order to solve a problem, if at all possible. Development work, on the other hand, requires the design, construction and completion of a unit to fulfil a certain task and meet a certain specification.

Cambridge Consultants was established in a disused bakery in 1961 and in its first year or so concentrated almost exclusively on the construction of prototypes. Soon the emphasis changed from the construction of prototypes to the design and construction of new processes or products to meet the requirements of customers. Recently there have been many projects in which the company saw the need for an innovation, conceived the fundamental principles that might meet the need, demonstrated the feasibility of this idea with a working model, then sold the expensive development and engineering stage to an industrial or government sponsor.

The problems which they have tackled are very diverse: to devise means of enabling a dentist to drill parallel holes in teeth; to measure the volume of coal in a 40' cube bunker by a contactless technique; to devise a system for making patterned carpets thirty times faster; to build equipment for automatically compiling a 600 volume index of all the library books in North America; to recommend fields of diversification for a mining equipment company and a precision mechanism company; to design low cost video tape equipment. These are some examples: there have also been scores of complex electronic assignments. An average contract lasts about six months and costs the sponsor about £2,500 – the size of contracts is, however, increasing steadily.

As with many other contract research groups there have been more ideas than sponsors and considerable success has been achieved in finding finance for setting up manufacturing organizations to make and sell the products where it was not possible to find a sponsor. These manufacturing organizations make electronic instruments, HiFi amplifiers, psychological apparatus, textile machinery. By mid-1969 the Group employed about a hundred and fifty people, more than a quarter of them with graduate qualifications, with a turn-over approaching £450,000 a year. This rate of growth involved a doubling in size every fifteen months throughout its history. Not surprisingly, and considering the antecedents of the operation, profits are totally re-invested in new projects rather than distributed as dividends for share holders.

This policy of ploughing back profits into internally initiated development work has prevented the accumulation of working capital to finance the operation and therefore about £100,000 worth of capital has had to be injected in the form of equity or loan stock. None the less, those who work for the company still hold about fifty per cent of its equity and their close relatives a further twenty five per cent.

The company is dependent entirely on the calibre of the men that it attracts. Its directors are aged thirty and the average age of members of the company is about twenty-eight. With this very small age range it is perhaps inevitable that there is an unusual and welcome status-avoiding structure. Every engineer who needs an office has a cell measuring 6' × 8'. Anyone in the firm is welcome to hire a small cheap van at £1 a week (tax and insurance extra). These are used as second vehicles by older married men, first by students. The whole company uses christian names and when a privilege has to be awarded it is accorded to the group that works the longest hours.

The whole operation of Cambridge Consultants appears to be geared round an intimate mixture of applied logic and inbuilt enthusiasm. When the management group couldn't decide the best priorities for 'perks' and benefits, the whole firm was asked to vote on the subject. Votes were weighed according to pay since highly paid people are the hardest to replace. At midnight there are as often as not people still working in the labs. The coffee machine is free since time costs 8d a minute (a charging rate of £2 per hour), and a minute may easily be wasted finding a 3d or 6d piece. 'May as well charge people for visiting the loo, which costs us considerably more.'

There are no time clocks but all grades of staff keep hourly time sheets. Everyone also receives overtime since it is not felt reasonable to saddle two men with enough work for three and then not to pay them for the long hours that this entails.

Pay, before overtime, is calculated to fall in the upper twenty-five per cent range for men of the relevant age and background. This is perhaps a little less than some could earn elsewhere, particularly as most of the engineers work a 45–55 hour week. However, the long hours are probably an indication of enthusiasm and commitment.

This freebooting atmosphere is not without its tougher side. Each job has to be costed every week; each quotation needs to be reviewed independently and costed according to a probability-estimate system by five different engineers; a man has only a matter of six months in which to become an invaluable contributor to the whole set-up or he is likely to be asked to find another job. Each senior man has a 'profit-centre' and has to meet a fairly tough budgeted growth in his sales and profit so few people can sleep easily if their projects reach a critical condition. However, staff turnover (defined as the loss of valued personnel) is very low and the growth rate achieved would be very respectable indeed even for a group that had not elected to tackle two of the toughest and most disciplined fields of engineering.

The group has developed its own special test to measure 'drive' as a counterbalance to I.Q. tests. Every engineer who joins the company is expected to pay his way by contributing paid time to his profit-centre. However, after achieving this, the profit-centre is encouraged to develop its own interest.

One of the most unusual aspects of Cambridge Consultants is that they act as a catch-pot for other teams of engineers who wish to go it alone. The company doesn't provide much backing but it does take on such a team and pay a salary to enable the team to seek its own backing.

To cater for all these different activities Cambridge Consultants has established a holding company structure and now has an interest in a dozen different enterprises which vary from wholly owned to three per cent participation. All of these companies promise to do well or outstandingly. Only two enterprises in which they have interested themselves have proved unsuccessful (though both continue to trade).

One of the most interesting facets of the science based production companies which they have launched is the dominance of brains as compared with brawn. The cost of a typical product is made up thus:

Raw material and stock keeping		25%
Unskilled labour and associated overheads	3%	
Semi-skilled labour and associated overheads	10%	
Skilled labour and associated overheads	12%	
Total production labour and overheads	25%	25%
Marketing, customer education, and management labour and associated overheads		25%
Research, Development and Profit		25%
		100%

It will be seen that the unskilled labour force is negligible and even the semi-skilled labour force, together with its overhead, is only accounting for ten per cent of the cost.

Another unusual aspect of the organization is that the 'literate engineer' is employed to undertake all the tasks of management except accounting. The company's house magazine bristles with parodies of writers such as James Joyce, A. A. Milne and Iris Murdoch, and with satirical descriptions of the behaviour of the various personnel – the directors receiving considerably more satirical attention than any other grades.

Cambridge Consultants appear to have gone some way towards finding a formula for bridging several of the 'gaps' that beset Britain today. Thus the management gap is bridged to some degree by a concentration or logical approach; the development gap, since this is a chosen field; and the 'entrepreneurial gap' by the science-based companies that have been launched. Whether at the end of the day Cambridge Consultants will achieve what are described as their 'disgustingly ambitious aims' will depend on maintaining the impetus that has been established. In a world where technology is changing so rapidly there is a double logistic problem: firstly, one must harness the abilities of young engineers before they become obsolescent and, secondly, one must keep their abilities and motivation razor-sharp for three or four decades after the engineer graduates. This particular problem is the one that Cambridge Consultants feel capable of solving now and in the future. Perhaps they may prove to have been among the first to do so.

11

Ingredients of Failure

COMPANY X

IMAGINE a group of three senior executives gathered in the boardroom of Company X on a wintry Monday morning. The Chairman is maintaining that the Company has never made a really good product. This is an attitude not uncharacteristic of quite a number of Company Chairmen who seem to get an almost masochistic – or maybe it is a sadistic – pleasure from offering destructive criticism. He is having a go at the Managing Director about this; the latter is something of a defeatist but defends the Company's products stubbornly arguing that the former Board ruined the range after the last war. The General Sales Manager, a genial optimist, is full of confidence. He doesn't agree. He feels that the products can't be too bad because he has lately had an excellent order from a large and developing retail chain called Multistore Ltd. But his anxiety is that he hasn't got anybody really competent to handle such a contact and sees himself, as usual, having to cope. The General Production Manager was in the factory 250 miles away. Had he been in this gloomy meeting he would have contradicted everybody and lost his temper.

As a result of this meeting it was decided to call in the help of an outside adviser who would see the problem objectively and would, if it were not already too late, make recommendations of a constructive nature.

Company X, making branded consumer goods, had once been leader in its field and was still well known. When it asked for outside help, however, the fourth successive trading loss had been announced, the dividend was in arrears, and bankers were exchanging glances.

The decline was the result of bad management past and present. The Board – Chairman, Managing Director, and three part-time directors – had been in office for two years. It had taken over after the shareholders had expelled the previous Board. The two senior members kept tight central control over the Company. Its recovery was prevented by the weaknesses in their management methods and was typified in the particular meeting that has been described.

1. Lack of Leadership

The Board had inherited a difficult situation. Quality had been debased to enable quick profits to be made in the sellers' market. When supplies became more plentiful this policy had rightly rebounded hard enough to unseat the old Board.

The new directors had the level of quality restored and awaited results. They did not come. The Chairman thus blamed the factory, the Managing Director his predecessors, and each privately blamed the other.

The fault, in such a situation, lay with both. The only hope of success was to give confident leadership to the Company and especially to the sales side. In this competitive market a minority of discriminating buyers knew that the products were good; the rest had a prejudice against the Company which only inspired salesmanship could overcome. Inspiration is not often a self-generated quality. To sit in Head Office criticizing the product or those formerly responsible for it is not the stuff of inspiration. Unusually able and enthusiastic leaders might have overcome the history of the product, but these men were frightened.

They also disagreed among themselves. The General Production Manager, in particular, took as little notice of the Board's authority as he could. He dismissed their suggestions on changes in the products as impractical, whether or not they were; he tried to introduce new lines and new packs by presenting the *fait accompli* rather than the suggestion; he pressed for costly machinery regardless of the financial state of the Company. Since he was an able man, he was retained. It would have been better, from the point of view of the Board's ability to lead, had he gone.

2. *Lack of Middle Management*

The strength of a company lies partly in the calibre of its leaders but at least as much in the quality of the men being trained to succeed them. If there is a wide gap between top management and the next tier of executives the result is usually that matters which should be delegated are not. Top management then tends to spend too much time on relatively simple tasks when it ought to be planning.

This was revealed in the General Sales Manager's comment. He was a splendid salesman himself. No one else could handle the Multistore account and no one else was being trained to do so. Thus he and, in their own spheres, other senior managers, were carrying out the duties of skilled men in the ranks below them. They were not spreading their vision wide, as managers must. They were merely doing better what they used, as junior executives, to do well.

3. *Lack of Perspective*

The salesman takes to the field on Monday, intelligence and emotions vibrating at the week's prospects. On Tuesday he breaks into a new market; and on Saturday, reporting on the week, the short week, he announces with delight that Multistore has given him an order.

The good Sales Manager is equally delighted. But the good Sales Manager sees wider than the new account and farther back than last week. He uses statistics as much as he uses personality.

It is, therefore, with a certain heaviness that one hears

a manager citing special cases to support a general statement. This is, perhaps, the most common failing of sales management in this country. In place of cool analysis of the location and correction of weaknesses in the overall sales the Sales Manager's function is too often seen as being that of star salesman.

The manager of a sales force of any size should be able to delegate any account to some man trained to handle it efficiently. He himself should visit customers only to keep in touch with the market or to give special weight, as a senior negotiator, when a particularly important deal is being arranged.

His main task is that of a strategist and not a brilliant guerrilla fighter.

4. *False Economy in Wages*

The labour turnover in the firm's sales force was about sixty per cent a year. General lack of faith in the Company was one factor behind this; lack of contact between the Board and the employees was another. By far the most important reason, however, was the practice of engaging salesmen at a very low salary and paying a rate of commission on all business which was enough to give a first-class representative no more than a comfortable income.

One of the most invaluable sales forces in the country consists of men earning on average more than £2,000 a year, and this in a highly competitive market. There is no greater mistake than to appear to want men to leave after they have served their purpose. Good men do not join firms whose atmosphere is cynical. Of those that do, the best are the first to go.

5. *Lack of Planning*

It follows, from the catalogue above, that this Company was not following a plan of development. It did not look ahead even in the short term. It had no budget. Sales followed a seasonal pattern and raw materials were bought at particular times of the year. Nevertheless there was no forecast of the cash position at different periods, and the firm was frequently short of money for purchases. Half a season's requirements might be bought at one time, and the advantage of bulk purchasing practically lost.

It would be reassuring to some extent if this were a caricature of bad management, but it is not. Some of the firm's faults were cured fairly rapidly. Others lasted as long as the Company.

The first task was to establish that the products were suitable for the market and knowledgeable buyers confirmed that they were.

The next stage was to re-establish confidence in a sales force which had lost faith in itself over many years. A revised scale of payments was introduced, consisting of a higher salary and a lower rate of commission, with a substantial increase in payments on the achievement of a high target level of sales. This enabled the firm to attract a better calibre of salesman, and gave the senior men a strong incentive to expand turnover.

For the first time recruits to the sales force were given training, not only in sales techniques, but in the history of the Company and in the way in which it worked. They met the Board, the managers, and the office staff to whom their orders and correspondence would be sent. The third stage was to plan the deployment of the force. From the Census of Distribution a picture was constructed of the number, size, and location of the retail outlets for the Company's products. Representatives were set a norm of a number of calls each week based on the performance of a good area. The number required in each part of the country was thus calculated.

It was found that some areas were considerably overstaffed. The poor performance of some of the junior men in the past was not, in fact, their fault. They had been given territories too small so support them. Through natural wastage, therefore, it was possible to reduce the force by almost one-third.

The drawing up of a sales budget, and hence a financial budget, was a simple matter. The Company had kept detailed sales records by product and by representative. The trade association to which the firm belonged published excellent and up-to-date information about the market. It was necessary only to put to use the raw data, which had accumulated in filing cabinets for some years.

These were the principal improvements which could be made fairly quickly. To teach the General Sales Manager to operate as a manager was a lengthy task. To convince the Board that, under their leadership, the Company could recover was lengthier. Neither task was completed: for after a time the reduction in the cost of selling and the increase in sales resulting from the improved payments system combined to give the Company some cash in hand. And when this happy state was reached it was taken over.

The moral is surely clear. Some thought-out marketing management after the new directors had assumed responsibility would have anticipated the final anti-climax – the take-over. There was nothing in the basic product range, or indeed in the Company's reputation, which could not have saved the day had the management – and this point is developed in the chapter 'The Business of Business' –thought ahead, remembering that the top management's job is to free itself from day-to-day decisions in order to concentrate on the longer term.

COMPANY Z

The case histories of successful management in the previous chapter spoke for themselves. Although there is some variation of product and service – electronics, catering, and retailing differ widely in scope – certain 'good' management factors are common to all the histories. Enlightened leadership and defined objectives, recognition of the problems to be tackled (and the maximum practicable inclusion of 'lower-down-the-line' managers in the planning) as well as a flexible approach to organizational requirements – these could fairly be described as the chief ingredients in the success recipe.

*

The following case history – as fictitious as the tale of Company X – deals with an imaginary Company Z which manufactures and retails quick-turnover branded consumer goods. To nominate a particular field of consumer goods would be invidious and irrelevant. Company Z has its own factory in London manufacturing a speciality 'own brand' range which is confined to its chain of 350 shops sited throughout the United Kingdom. These shops also retail a wide range of publicly advertised goods in the same field which are competitive with Company Z's 'own brand'. There is a Head Office and warehouse both of which are also situated in London. The company, which employs in all about 1,700 people, is now a public one, although the majority of the shares are held by one family which, since the Company started nearly a hundred years ago, under dynamic leadership has provided the Board of Directors.

The ingredients of failure that will be set down in this story are taken from a wide cross-section of much of British business and are, unfortunately, all too frequently to be found. That this imaginary Company Z is still making reasonable profits and would not, to a superficial eye, seem to have the seeds of decay within it, is not surprising. But Company Z is in a fool's paradise; unless it speedily mends its ways the factors of bad management that will emerge as this case history develops will gradually destroy a hitherto not unsuccessful operation. At this moment in time, in a fairly robust economy, making and dispensing merchandise the consumption of which essentially reflects 'good times', the Board of Company Z might well feel that a Cassandra prophesying woe (should such a prophet ever get the Board's ear) is talking rubbish. He could, however, be proved right, and sooner than Company Z realizes.

The organizational structure of Company Z is extremely confused, a patchwork quilt that has been added to from time to time. Attempts to clarify the structure have, since they have only been half-hearted and piecemeal, added to the confusion. Any changes are made solely as a matter of expediency to accommodate an exceptional person, either strong or weak, at a given moment; they then become absorbed into tradition, so the structure never reverts to normal.

There is no clear line of command to the retail shops; although they are notionally responsible to a shops controller he has little authority other than for 'rations and discipline'. Each of the several departmental controllers at headquarters – in charge of supplies, building, personnel, or administrative function – can issue a direct order to a shop manager. If relations are amicable he may put the order through the shops controller or at least inform him of his intentions; only too often, relations are strained or the departmental controller is of a higher status, so that the order goes direct. In this the departmental controller is acting not in a staff but in a command capacity; he has, by implied consent – no specific terms of reference have ever been formulated or written – complete authority for his actions, and he frequently proceeds without discussing his intentions with any of the other departmental controllers; no formal means of communication between these controllers have ever been laid down and members of the Board make a great point of never seeing two controllers simultaneously. The result of this is that the poor shop manager has several bosses, all issuing commands (often conflicting) and all demanding priority.

This, then, is the organizational structure, considerably simplified – a basically simple retail operation with specialist functions cutting across it and a factory operation serving all outlets. It is interesting to observe that one of the case studies of 'Recipes for Success' advocates just such a structure and has found, in practice, that the dreaded disadvantages of overlapping have not materialized. Why is this so? Why is this recipe not a successful sauce for this present gander? The answer probably lies in size, age, and quality. The successful management, Laws Stores, controls fifty-two branches and 400 employees – Company Z has many more branches and employees plus a factory. Laws Stores is fifty years old but still only in the second generation – Company Z is nearly 100 years old and has suffered several generations. Finally, and the most important of all, is the quality of management, a topic to be considered at greater length later. Laws Stores still has its original founder, an obviously dynamic man, as its Chairman; he has shortened his span of control and introduced new techniques of management to help him achieve this, but still injects his own personality and enthusiasm into the business; he has introduced a new generation of executives with a mixture of 'inside' and 'outside' experience. Company Z was started by just such a founder but his firm hand and energetic leadership have long been absent; his followers have not unnaturally been of smaller stature, but they have made little coherent attempt to replace the drive and know-how of one man by normal management techniques whereby they might draw upon the accumulated knowledge and experience of their many assistants; above all, they have been unimaginative in their choice of executives, and have promoted only from the

'inside' on the basis of long service from amongst men with
no knowledge of training for general management.

Moving further up the organization, from the departmental level to the Board, there is even greater confusion of
command. The Board has never fully recognized the fact
that it is no longer one man running a business of moderate
size, so that no satisfactory management techniques have
been evolved to enable it to watch the progress of each sector
of the business or to control and direct it through professional managers and functional specialists. Instead, after
meeting and deliberating as a Board, each member of it has
a generalized responsibility for one or more of the functional
departments, with the apparently understood proviso that no
decision of the Board as a whole should be binding upon him
individually! To introduce a further hazard, each member
of the Board circulates throughout the country inspecting
the branches and is liable to make a snap decision contrary
to all previously agreed policy. Chaos is prevented only by
the senior departmental controllers meeting as an informal
committee and deciding a common line of action. It is also
a fairly simple game to 'play off' one member of the Board
against another; an unpalatable decision by a director in his
capacity as a departmental director is easily avoided by
waiting until he is away for a few days and then putting the
problem to his temporary 'stand-in', another director whose
contrary sympathies are well known.

The Quality of Management

It is often said that an organization can be no better than
the men in it. In Company Z the organization gets the
calibre of the man that it deserves.

The calibre of top management in the foregoing paragraphs on the organization has already been touched upon.
The directors are all drawn from the family of the original
founder, or from other families which have either married

into the business, or which have been brought in to assist on the basis of a school, university, or army friendship. There is no competition for a directorship; if a son wishes to enter the business, instead of law or medicine, he is free to do so – whether or not he enters the business he will be assured of a substantial income from it. Admittedly, having made this decision, his training within the company will be thorough; he will be put through the factory and may do a stint in a shop, but none of the present or potential directors has had any professional, technical, or business training and precisely because the trainee is 'family' there is a danger that the basic indoctrination will be somewhat perfunctory.

Apart from this training of pre-selected directors, there is no route to the Board through the business. The highest appointment to which an 'other rank' can aspire is Departmental Manager; no Departmental Manager, however brilliant or well-versed in the business, has ever been appointed to the Board – not even the man who is nominally in charge of the factory. Equally, no case has been known of an injection of strength into the Board by the appointment of a person with professional qualifications or experience or with a successful background in another business.

At the next level of management, heads of departments and their assistants, are all, without exception, promoted within the business, mostly from the people who have spent the whole of their working lives since the age of fourteen within it. They have had no training for management and most of them would ridicule the idea that they might benefit by training; none are aware that facilities for executive education and discussion exist. That they are, therefore, extremely limited in outlook is hardly surprising; indeed it is a great tribute to their inborn qualities and their determination that they have done so well. The fault lies in management that such men are so ill prepared for the positions they have won. Most have developed a flair for discipline and administrative routine, but they are not always the most tactful when dealing with the ranks from which they have been promoted; they have acquired a multitude of facts relating to the business which have been invaluable to them in a junior capacity, but now they are not equipped to assess the broader aspects of the business. A typical example of this is a department manager who can remember the names and addresses of all suppliers, the volume of trade done with each over the past twenty years and the amount lost through bad buys; this is quite a feat for there are a good many suppliers.

Continuing down the scale, there are fewer criticisms to be made of the quality of the junior managers, such as shop managers or the works and transport manager in the factory. Here the size of the command has reached the calibre of person available. Management at this level is not imaginative nor is it expected to be. Until recently, application, diligence, reliability, and accuracy were the qualities most demanded and the scope of these managers was so restricted that only a person of fairly low intelligence and initiative was attracted to the work; there is still no breeding or forcing ground for potential senior managers and this is one of the most serious weaknesses of the organization.

Staff Relationships

Company Z prides itself on its staff relationships and has, in fact, been a pioneer of welfare services. Unfortunately, in spite of this, the morale of staff is steadily declining; the wastage in staff is steadily increasing, recruitment is becoming more difficult, and the directors are at a loss to understand the reason for these trends.

There are, of course, many reasons contributing to this state of affairs, some merely typical of the difficulties experienced by all employers, but others which are within the control of the company. The primary failing is the lack of personnel policy which, in turn, is probably due to lack of awareness of the conditions of today. The general control of personnel matters is in the hands of the Board, an assistant to the directors, who deals with staff welfare schemes, and a personnel officer, who was appointed to conform to current practice, but without any clear ideas or mandate as to what his duties should be. Thus there are three principal spokesmen; add to this the facts that each operational departmental manager is reluctant to accept guidance and that the Board itself does not speak as one body, but is liable to spark off in any direction at the whim of an individual, and it is clear that a coordinated personnel policy is impossible.

That there is a lack of appreciation of current conditions is not surprising. The three personnel officers have had no training in personnel matters and certainly do not intend to start training at their late age; they do no reading on the subject and have few contacts with their counterparts in other companies, following the usual principle that 'outside' experience has no bearing on their own internal affairs. The directors whose voices carry the most weight in staff matters went through their training at about the time of the First World War, and spent their formative period as active executive directors during the twenties; the staff relationships of this period are indelibly imprinted in their outlook. At this time, in fact almost up to the beginning of the Second World War, a managership of a shop represented a safe, comfortable, and respectable – almost white-collar – job which was open to anyone with limited educational attainments and no special training. Now the conditions are rapidly changing; staff seek responsibility and prospects, not safety; there are new techniques in retailing, a challenge which can only be met by knowledge, energy, and dynamism at branch level; above all, there must be staff participation in new schemes and a 'feed-back' of information and ideas from the shop floor. It is this feature which is totally lacking under the feudalistic outlook of the Board. Communications pass only from the top to the bottom; assistance is not sought nor is criticism tolerated.

On the other side of the business, in the factory, there is an inability to cope with militant unionism. Union representatives are rarely taken into the management's confidence and there is an atmosphere of distrust on both sides. Again there is no policy, only expediency; any major issue is, if possible, shelved or postponed rather than faced; there is constant bickering over minor issues in the fear that an unexpected precedent might be established.

Research and Development

The deep-rooted reluctance to change is perhaps best illustrated by the company's attitude to research and development. The retail side, which is more progressive than the factory and Head Office administrative sides of the business has undertaken a reasonable amount of research into selling methods, leading to proposals for new display techniques and self-service; implementation of these proposals has, however, been extremely slow, largely owing to the multi-headed departmental structure – so many departments are affected by a proposed change that it is rare to achieve agreement, particularly as the heads of departments, being firmly entrenched in the Head Office, have expanded themselves to a higher stature than the men outside.

A very limited use is made of organization and methods techniques. One of the directors was told in his Golf Club that O. & M. was the modern word in business, so an O. & M. section was formed; indeed, several suitable young men were recruited and trained; but they soon left when they saw that the section would not be allowed to do any useful work. The first obstacle has been the directors' persistent refusal to understand the subject or to find out anything about it; they are still convinced that it is a new way of preparing accounts. Heads of departments are quick to sense the lack of backing, and have so far managed to block most worthwhile proposals; one scheme had been developed and agreed on paper to the point where a pilot run was suggested. 'A pilot run?' said the relevant controller. 'That means you have no confidence in your proposals. They either go in in full or not at all.' The scheme went in, and was a success, but suffered in the early stages from the lack of a debugging period which would have considerably eased its progress. This episode emphasizes one of the shortcomings of so many Z companies which are not founded on a skilled trade or on any technical – e.g. scientific or engineering – knowledge; the staff have had no experience of learning, other than learning the existing details of the business; there are no trained observers, no experimentation; none of them knows the teething troubles which any new project must go through before it is made into a success; as one manager might put it – 'I am not interested in introducing anything into my department which is not already a proved success.'

There is no work study or method study. The only persons known to have observed working methods objectively and to have put forward proposals for eliminating wasted effort both in the factory and the shops are the local representatives of the main unions involved; these were, of course, ignored, since the findings reflected on the efficiency of the departmental head and since any proposal from the union was automatically suspect.

There is a large distribution problem, with about 350 branches (sinks) and many alternative points of dispatch (sources), but the company steadfastly refuses to allow any systematic analysis of this problem to be made. The techniques of operational research might well point to substantial savings in the cost of distribution.

Summing up, therefore, little use is made of the modern aids to management such as market research, work study, organization and methods, operational research, or management accounting, and where they are used they are largely ineffective owing to lack of top-level backing, lack of appreciation of the subjects throughout the managerial ranks, and, most devastating of all, refusal to learn.

Summing Up

The melancholy story of Company Z has been written in order to present some ingredients of failure. These have, therefore, been emphasized, and the case history has ignored a great deal that is good. The company has had a successful history of expansion, was responsible for many innovations and even today is performing a useful public service and providing stable employment for a sizeable number of people. The ingredients of failure are becoming, however, increasingly evident and, unless action is taken, the bad will drive out the good. Recapitulating, the main ingredients are:

1. There is a reluctance to experiment and change in order to meet the challenge of new ways. Although every change in social habits and in transportation was anticipated and exploited in the early days of the company and during its expansion, there is now a feeling that the old ways were best. The revolution in our social structure and outlook, particularly since the last war, is not only ignored – it is not even known to exist.

2. The reluctance to change is a direct consequence of management failure. The directors, although drawn largely from his descendants, no longer resemble the thrusting entrepreneur who built up the business; they have moved up into 'society', are more concerned with social and sporting events than with the more sordid details of business administration. Such men are in no hurry to change an established institution that has afforded them so much comfort throughout

their lives; they did not see the beginnings, born with truly imaginative zest, and they cannot see the decay which is inevitable if the outlook remains static; nothing must be done to hazard the security of the present – their only safety lies in the experience of the past. Little new thought or leadership from the top is possible under these circumstances, and the executive stratum is quick to reflect this outlook.

3. There is a wide gulf between the directors and executives and employees. Before the First World War this did not matter – was even an advantage; between the wars the seeds of doubt were sown; now the management has no following amongst the 'lower orders'.

4. Staff consultation is unknown. Any member of the staff, either in the Head Office, the factory, or out in the field, is expected to do anything, go anywhere, and may be expected to uproot his home and move at no notice; there is some surprise that some of the junior staff have put out roots and have problems like children's education to consider. Ideas are never sought from the staff; at all levels of junior and senior management it would be undignified to seek advice from a lower level.

5. Good men are not retained. Promotion is slow. Steady, reliable types are preferred for the executive strata – indeed, no one with drive and imagination stays long enough to be considered for a top post. Directorships are, as they always have been, open only to members of the family or family connexions. Although the training of the lower grades of shop assistant is quite good, there is no training for general management, and no rotation of staff between the retailing, factory, and administrative sides of the business to give a promising young man an overall view.

6. No comprehensive plans are made for the future. The company has been built up and expanded as a matter of expediency – has, in fact, flourished on expediency. Why should it not continue in this way?

7. The size of the organizational unit has grown too large for the calibre of man available to control it.

Here, then are some of the ingredients of failure. How is it that they are present in many companies which are to all external appearances successful and which have not yet failed?

It is true, as was said at the beginning of this case history, that such a company is in a fool's paradise. The tempo of business is increasing and new management methods, both tangible and intangible, are challenging complacency.

There are still too many businesses in Great Britain which are resting on the laurels of the past and living in the days of their forefathers.

12

Management Tomorrow

THIS closing chapter is really an extension of the earlier one on management development. The men and women who are learning today will be leading tomorrow. There is a great deal of current speculation about the kind of people who are going to be required to cope with the management situations that will assuredly emerge as the new technologies enable more and more of the routine, mechanical part of most business operations to be done by fewer and fewer. 'Management development' for all the somewhat austere implications of the phrase is, and rightly so, a mid-twentieth-century business preoccupation.

The point surely is that people do not change all that much. It is unlikely that a new 'breed' of manager is going to emerge. What *is* certain is that vastly different situations will have to be managed and thus, as human nature is not as subject to violent change as human achievement, there is more relevance in thinking about the climate of tomorrow's management challenge rather than about those men and women who will be expected to accept it.

As vivid a means as any of examining the problem of tomorrow is to put down an imagined dialogue. The *dramatis personae* are the former Works Manager of Company A and his closest friend, who is a schoolmaster. The ex-Works Manager is thirty-six, ambitious and energetic. He was earning a good salary, had a reasonable amount of responsibility, but was avid for more. He married young and has three children at school; he pays for the education of the two eldest, but has decided that the youngest, who is nine, can take advantage of the State educational system as he feels he is already paying too many taxes and that No. 3 can forfeit whatever it is the other two are getting. He is a mechanical engineer, an A.M.I.Mech.E. in fact, with a good mind, and he has opted for the wider horizon of top management. Convinced that his former company, a solid, family-owned Midland engineering works, will plod along over the next twenty years, but will never do anything really imaginative about new methods and technologies, he has, despite his wife's misgivings, thrown in his hand, forfeited the Company's contributions to the pension scheme to which he has been contributing for a good many years, and is momentarily without a job. He knows quite well that he will eventually get one; the question is: what sort of company with what kind of attitudes to the future is he seeking? His salary at the time of his somewhat abrupt decision was £3,500 a year, plus a car, reasonable expenses, and a deduction of five per cent which was his contribution to the Company's superannuation scheme. Other 'fringe benefits', as they have come to be awkwardly known, did not exist in his former company; housing loans, for example, were not granted and there were no schemes of employee participation in profits either by bonus, profit-sharing arrangements, or employee shares.

He has confidence in himself and really wants to be a Top Person, but he is neither priggish nor vain. A product of grammar school, military service (R.E.M.E.), shop-floor apprenticeship, and part-time studies at a local Technical College, he is as much interested in people as in things. He feels, quite genuinely, that he has flair for 'man management' and that he wants that kind of management to cover a wider field than the running of a works. He longs to be in on *total* policy and *total* planning.

His friend, who was at school with him, won a scholarship to Oxford and read classics. He is short-sighted and was excused military service. By nature reserved and a shade

cynical he has become, however, an effective and an enlightened schoolmaster. He is a bachelor and takes a detached view of life. Always a little sceptical of 'business' and
business motives he is nevertheless fascinated by a world that
he knows he could never endure. He reads the *Economist*
and, lately, he has been advising seventeen-year-olds about
'careers' at the school at which he teaches; so he is (without
showing it) passionately interested in, and not a little admir-
ing of, his friend's boldness in throwing a fairly expensive
bonnet over the windmill.

They are sitting in two fairly comfortable chairs in the
saloon bar of a public-house in a town in the Midlands. The
angry young ex-Works Manager is called Ted; the schoolmaster, Derek.

TED (testily): Of course I know just what you are thinking, Derek – you're convinced that I'm mad to give up a
good job with even a possibility of getting on to the Board
when the old man dies. I know all that, but can't you see
that I've got to be in an outfit where there is some looking
ahead?

DEREK (placidly): Methinks you do protest too much. I
never said you were mad. What I said was that I don't believe you've sorted out two questions. Is it simply that you're
in such a darned hurry or do you honestly think that your
old lot will eventually fall by the wayside and that you must
find a firm that will have the right ideas for the future?
What I am really trying to say is: are you being reasonably
detached about this? – or are you just impatient?

TED (thoughtfully): That's a fair comment. I agree that I
want to get on but, honestly, I saw no health in my old company. Let me try to explain – and I hope this won't sound
like double-dutch to a dim schoolmaster. There is no question but that methods are changing at a terrific speed these
days and will change even quicker over the next ten years.

To take one example. I couldn't get my people to invest in an automatic lathe. I wasn't suggesting a particularly expensive or fancy piece of equipment, but we have been turning off standard shafts for many years on a couple of old centre lathes. What I couldn't make them see was that, although the old machines had been written down to nothing and were really scrap in any case, a new automatic lathe would save at least £30 a week in labour and scrap and would not cost the company more than £2,500. Forgive the technicalities, but that's the sort of thing I mean.

DEREK: That sounds fair enough, but I suppose it is just arguable that your people felt so much was going on in the automation world – or so I gather from reading the *Economist* and hearing some of my boys discuss it – that anything they bought today might be obsolete tomorrow. Is this sense or am I talking though my hat?

TED (tolerantly): Of course there *is* a germ of truth in what you say but the Board ought at least to have been receptive to the idea of seeing what a modern machine tool might or might not have been able to do for us. I think the real trouble was that my former masters are terrified about redundancy and are scared of the Unions. What I couldn't get over to them – though they were always perfectly courteous and patient with me – was that the skilled operators in our kind of engineering works will always be required but in the future will be using their skills in different directions. So what I do feel is that the man on the shop floor in the very near future will be doing quite different sort of work; will have to be planning his work; will have different kinds of maintenance problems to tackle; and so on. We ought to have been getting prepared with a new kind of training for the day when most of the repetitive jobs will no longer be done by people. Do you get my drift?

DEREK: Yes, go on, I'm interested.

TED: I don't want to exaggerate this. The fact that my

people couldn't see that new equipment and new training were becoming important for them put some responsibility on me. I can see now that I ought to have battled much harder than I did but you know, Derek, there are times when it's hopeless and I think that was one of them. The family was fundamentally selfish – these are good times for smallish engineering businesses – and anything I said would have sounded unreal and impractical. I suppose I also lacked moral courage. I should have made more of an issue of it and I might have pulled it off, especially if I'd presented my case properly. Instead I packed it in – I hadn't really learnt how to manage myself! I remember reading somewhere that management tomorrow will need chaps who can see problems 'in the round', who must not be blinkered and who will appreciate the need for speed of decision. I *must* get myself into a Company whose prospects of development will eventually give me a chance to think in that sort of way. Management will be dealing with a completely new set of problems because, by and large, the routine, unskilled worker will have largely ceased to be.

DEREK: I wonder if you're really right. Do you honestly see industry's routines *all* being mechanized? Won't there always be a mass of humdrum jobs for humdrum men and girls to do, and isn't there, for a long time yet, plenty of scope for managers in seeing that the jobs are made as interesting as possible?

I remember a really horrifying book which came out in the early fifties called *The Making of a Moron* written by an American called Brennan. As a result of a survey the author showed that quite a number of jobs for which U.S.A. industry demanded fairly intelligent people could be done just as well by morons. What teachers call E.S.N. – educationally sub-normal.

TED: I believe you've got something there. Of course I can see that for ages yet there will be a need for human beings to do pretty dreary tasks – just think of insurance, banking, the Civil Service, retail distribution, and so on – they're bound to move more slowly towards automating themselves – but I do see, quite honestly, that in 1984 (saving Orwell's reputation) or thereabouts we might well see the overall business operation as a question of skilful management of things as much as people. That is why I want to be in an outfit that is thinking that way.

DEREK: It's a gruesome thought! Some people just won't be able to adapt themselves to these new challenges, won't want responsibility, and won't even respond to the sort of education and training that will have to prepare for the new conditions. What'll happen to them? Where will they go? Perhaps there'll be a return to the land!

TED: I don't believe you're taking me very seriously! What I'm trying to say is that of course there will be plenty of scope for conventional management (rather like conventional armaments!) for a long while to come. I think, on the whole, that these new managers, through experience and example, are coming along all the time. What is just as true, I think, is that a number of industries will alter tremendously – are in fact altering tremendously – with the arrival of the new technologies and that to manage the men who will be managing the constituent parts of such industries could be a really exciting job. That's what I want to do.

DEREK: Give me an example of the sort of industry you mean – I suppose you'll give me a manufacturing one because you are an engineer – but could I have one just the same?

TED: Let's see. I'm sure that a motor accessory plant could very quickly dispense with machine operators and could well become entirely automated. Or a process industry like oil refining. And only the other day I was hearing about a piston plant in Russia where the pistons aren't touched by hand from casting to packaging. There is going to be a great deal of management skill required to keep those sort of plants going but, my goodness, what a challenge.

DEREK: But tell me something – if we accept the basic idea (and I believe we both do) that human relationships are the most satisfying ones in the long term, how will this fit into your conception of the new sort of highly professional management? What place will there be for such relationships? Won't everything ultimately become clinical and remote?

TED: (stubbornly): I refuse to believe it. I think, in actual fact, that the business of making the most of the equipment that is becoming available, of planning for it and thus gradually removing the squalor and repetitiveness from human work, will give management an entirely new sense of responsibility. You may think this sounds hollow, but I mean it. I see future managers not as builders and maintainers of tiny little private empires but as cooperators in far more selfless enterprises.

DEREK: I think I see what you mean, but I'm still bothered about those millions who don't want, and never will want, to do much thinking for themselves. In agricultural economies like South-East Asia or large parts of Africa it may not be so serious a problem – though heaven knows the rest of the world has a responsibility for seeing that the peasant doesn't starve any more. But what about the industrial economies? One sees unemployment in quite a big way now in the United States. Is this because industrial methods have developed too fast? I don't know. I'm simply asking. Or here in the U.K. It's true we have pretty well full employment, but at what price? How long, in fact, will our economy stand the strain? Again, I confess I'm bothered about your vaunted technological progress because, whatever population statistics say or don't say, people are going to be born, will need to be protected, and will have to work. A bit of slowing down might be no bad thing, don't you think? And of course we must realize that near full employment in Great Britain means a good deal of concealed unemployment and that lots of people in every sort of business enterprise are not fully stretched. I'm sure there's a lot of idleness around and I often think it would be more honest to admit its existence, cut down working hours, and call it, without humbug, increased leisure.

Even so, isn't there a case for slowing down in some of the industries that are automating themselves so fast?

TED: No, Derek, you can't halt the processes. Not even war does that – ironically. In fact war as we now know it actually accelerates the processes. But this discussion has certainly crystallized one idea that has been floating around in my mind over the last year or two. It is this. I believe that the biggest future challenge to a manager – and I want to be in on the challenge – will be precisely to strike the balance between technological and human situations – to sacrifice, if necessary, a technical improvement if its adoption would cause real human hardship or, conversely, to have the courage, energy, and enthusiasm to work out new developments if one can see ahead to new requirements and new satisfactions. Management must surely be much more flexible than it has been in the past. It must not become enslaved by the new technologies, but it must be constantly looking at them and then accepting or rejecting them after considered judgement. Of course I see very well that it's a bit unreal to see all this in isolation. However enlightened a top manager you may want to be, the facts of international trade and competition, taxation, nuclear politics – a host of outside forces in fact – can bear tremendously on the issue. But I still don't think they subtract from the fascination of the new task. After all it is this business of making a proper adjustment between the individual and the aggregate – if that is a fair way to put it – that will distinguish and perhaps save us from the Communists. Management seems to me to have an enormous job to do here. On the one hand there are temptations of the mass market, of size for the sake of size and of efficiency for the sake of efficiency: on the other, an enduring belief that human dignity – in our case I think it's the respect of the manager for the managed and vice versa – is what matters. This has been quite a speech but I had to make it.

DEREK: Of course you did. And I'm happy to hear your enthusiasm. I think I see what you mean and I'm sure you're right to go on emphasizing that however technical and professional management may become, human factors will still be the priority. I respect the idea of the individuality and the essential dignity of Man. We must, I'm sure, hang on to that for all we are worth.

TED: I'm aware that when I find the right sort of job it'll none of it be as cut and dried as I've suggested. The character of future Management must obviously be a kind of compromise, because the claims of the individual and the claims of the future will be everlastingly running counter. But I see no need to be daunted by this, Derek, as long as you teachers give our children some sense of perspective and turn out at least a percentage who like responsibility and want to go for it. I won't pretend that there are solutions to this problem of technology *v.* humanity; all I can say is that I recognize that the problem exists, will exist more dramatically in the future, and that I want to have a crack at trying to solve it.

DEREK: Yes, but I think you've got to be a bit more precise. After all you're out of work at present and though I know you'll get fixed up quickly you can't afford to be too starry-eyed about all this can you?

Could I outline something I've often thought about and hear what you think? It's this: it has been fashionable to claim that the aims of the scientists and the humanitarians are diametrically opposed to each other and that technology and humanity, especially in business, are irreconcilable. But I wonder if this is really so. It seems to me that the scientists genuinely believe that technology will improve the human lot and we know that the humanitarians (not that I like the word much!) even if sceptical of too much technology, are clearly dedicated to bettering social conditions. The goals, in fact, are identical. The scientists – or should I say, the technologists – go about it systematically, while the non-scientists work on a pretty empirical basis believing that experience and compromise are better than too much detached planning. Where does management come into this? As I see it the manager, and particularly tomorrow's manager, will be the catalyst. It will be up to him or her to reduce the gap of misunderstanding between technicians and non-technicians so that both sorts of mind will work in an atmosphere of maximum cooperation. Do you agree?

TED: Yes, I do. This is just what I feel management to be all about and that is what I've really been trying to say since we started this discussion. The manager of tomorrow has somehow got to bridge that gap in the business operation which, at first sight, might seem to be unbridgeable. I think immediately of the pressing claims of a research and development staff in the teeth of the equally pressing argument from the financial boys who, inevitably, have to think of the shareholders. In the long term there is no particular conflict: the sound researcher and the sound accountant both want to see an efficient, viable operation, but the manager is perhaps the only one whose training and aptitude should fit him for striking the short-term balance. I think it's pretty well accepted nowadays that, as businesses become bigger and more complex, the technological aspects will become even larger. They must, because you cannot stop the inventors, the innovators, and the perfectionists. If this is so, the tendency for people to exaggerate the conflict will be greater, and so will the need for level-headed management.

Applying all this to my own case I would finally say this: the manager's job becomes more interesting every day, and I can't see why I should go bumbling along in a business enterprise which barely recognizes this fact. That's why I've taken this chance on myself, and why I must find a firm that sees its managers as the people on whom the future success of the business utterly depends.

And so on . . .

*

An imagined dialogue can only hope to capture a little of what younger people, on whose shoulders future management responsibilities must rest, are saying and thinking. In these troubled times when waste, squalor, lack of imagination, and greed are as much enemies of progress as threats, tensions, and tyrannies, the manager in a free society cannot afford the luxury of inertia. He must see himself as the spearhead in the battle against complacency, for, assuredly, it is the attitude of complacent people to tomorrow's demands that make management so exacting yet exciting a business.

Index

MORE ABOUT PENGUINS
AND PELICANS

Penguinews, which appears every month, contains details of all the new books issued by Penguins as they are published. From time to time it is supplemented by *Penguins in Print*, which is a complete list of all books published by Penguins which are in print. (There are well over three thousand of these.)

A specimen copy of *Penguinews* will be sent to you free on request, and you can become a subscriber for the price of the postage – 4s. for a year's issues (including the complete lists). Just write to Dept EP, Penguin Books Ltd, Harmondsworth, Middlesex, enclosing a cheque or postal order, and your name will be added to the mailing list.

Some other books published by Penguins are described on the following pages.

Note: *Penguinews* and *Penguins in Print* are not available in the U.S.A. or Canada

PROGRESS OF MANAGEMENT RESEARCH

EDITED BY NIGEL FARROW

'Management research,' writes Nigel Farrow, 'is science's Oliver Twist; a delicate and neglected infant of obscure parentage, it has been suddenly claimed by various competing godfathers for reasons ranging from disinterested charity to commercial exploitation.'

This volume in the Pelican Library of Business and Management contains ten articles which originally appeared as a series in *Business Management*. It is a sign of the fluid state of management studies that the contributors include professors of marketing, business administration, industrial psychology, operational research, and industrial and management engineering, as well as economists and consultants. Covering the functional areas of production, personnel, finance, and marketing, they indicate the debt owed by business research to economics, mathematics, psychology, and sociology.

It remains a question whether management research does better to be wide, general, and abstract (a pursuit for academic cloisters); or specific, local, and concrete (an exercise for the oil-grimed shop). But in any case the recent research outlined in these essays is constructive and practical and never loses sight of the manager on the spot.

Pelican Library of Business and Management

COMPUTERS, MANAGERS AND SOCIETY

MICHAEL ROSE

Computers, Managers and Society is an account, part technical, part sociological and part philosophical, of the computer revolution.

After a general survey of the development of computer-controlled data processing, Michael Rose examines the complex effects of the computer upon the clerical worker – the new opportunities, the dangers of alienation, the threat of technological unemployment. He then focuses upon the fast-developing problems of managers. Many of the standard managerial functions can already be programmed. But should executives delegate qualitative decisions to a machine? And if so, how far can and should these changes go?

'Computerization' presents managers with new opportunities on a structural scale unmatched since the Industrial Revolution. Do they really understand the new situation? Can they, when it is transforming itself so rapidly? And are we enough aware of the effects of the computer upon an even larger social group – society itself – now faced with the need to clarify its whole attitude to technological change?